In
the
Storm
of
Roses

The Lockert Library
of Poetry in Translation

For other titles in the Lockert Library
see page 209

In the Storm of Roses

Selected Poems by Ingeborg Bachmann

TRANSLATED, EDITED, AND INTRODUCED BY

MARK ANDERSON

PRINCETON
UNIVERSITY PRESS

Copyright © 1986 by Princeton University Press
Published by Princeton University Press, 41 William Street, Princeton,
New Jersey 08540
In the United Kingdom: Princeton University Press, Guildford, Surrey

All Rights Reserved

Library of Congress Cataloging in Publication Data will be found on the last printed
page of this book

ISBN 0-691-06672-8 (cloth)
       01428-0 (pbk.)

The German text of the poems is taken from *Ingeborg Bachmann. Werke*, vol. 1,
Gedichte, Hörspiele, Libretti, Überzetungen, © 1978 R. Piper & Co. Verlag

The Lockert Library of Poetry in Translation is supported by a bequest from Charles
Lacy Lockert (1888-1974)

This book has been composed in Linotron Bodoni
Clothbound editions of Princeton University Press books are printed on acid-free
paper, and binding materials are chosen for strength and durability.
Paperbacks, although satisfactory for personal collections, are not usually
suitable for library rebinding
Printed in the United States of America by Princeton University Press
Princeton, New Jersey

DESIGNED BY LAURY A. EGAN

Contents

Translator's Note	ix
Introduction: Poet on the Border	3

FROM THE COLLECTION
Mortgaged Time

Leaving Port	27
Departure from England	31
Fall, My Heart	33
Dark Words	35
Paris	37
The Heavy Freight	39
Autumn Maneuver	41
Mortgaged Time	43
Wood Chips	45
Early Noon	49
Every Day	53
Message	55
The Bridges	57
Night Flight	59
Psalm	63
In the Storm of Roses	67
Salt and Bread	69
Great Landscape near Vienna	73

FROM THE COLLECTION
Invocation of the Great Bear

The Game Is Over	81
Invocation of the Great Bear	85
My Bird	87
A New Land	91

Curriculum Vitae	93
Land of Fog	101
Tell Me, Love	105
Advertisement	109
Word and Afterword	111
The Firstborn Land	115
Songs from an Island	117
Night Portrait of Rome	125
In Apulia	127
Shadow Roses Shadow	129
Stay	131
To the Sun	133
Songs of Flight	137

SELECTED LATER POEMS

[Don't prescribe any faith to this race]	157
Hôtel de la Paix	159
Exile	161
After This Deluge	163
Stream	165
Go, My Thought	167
Aria I	169
You Words	171
Truly	175
Bohemia Lies by the Sea	177
Prague January 64	181
A Kind of Loss	183
Enigma	185
No Delicacies	187

APPENDIX

Biographical Note	193

What I Saw and Heard in Rome	195
[On the Origin of the Title "In Apulia"]	201
[What Good Are Poems?]	203
The Poem for the Reader	205
Chronology	206

Translator's Note

THE PRESENT EDITION of Ingeborg Bachmann's poetry is based on the German edition of her collected works (*Werke*, Munich, R. Piper & Co. Verlag, 1978) and includes all poems that could be successfully rendered into English. Poems from Bachmann's youth, as well as intricately rhymed poems (such as the ten-part cycle "Von einem Land, einem Fluβ und den Seen") had to be omitted. This is unfortunate, for much of Bachmann's strength as a poet derives from her fusion of a contemporary idiom with a rigorously crafted, classical form. But the criterion for any verse translation must be that the poem work in its own language. This principle has guided the selection of the poems presented here. Several short prose works relating to Bachmann's poetry, as well as a biographical note and chronology, have been added as an appendix. They should facilitate access to her verse and may also whet the reader's taste for her prose works, few of which have been translated into English.

These translations are the work of more hands than my own. I am grateful to Heinz and Sheila Bachmann, who first saw enough merit in a primitive version of the manuscript to encourage me to improve it; they carefully reviewed the manuscript at two different stages, locating many errors and offering suggestions of their own. I would also like to thank Christine Koschel and Inge von Weidenbaum, Bachmann's friends and editors, who graciously answered my questions about the more obscure points of the German originals. Eva Geulen, Klaus Haberkamm, William McClain, and Rainer Nägele all lent a native or near-native ear to explain to me Bachmann's use of German. Jean McGarry worked in the other direction, counseling me when the original German obtruded too heavily on the poems in English. Two scholar-poets, Michael Fried and Richard Macksey, set a crucial example for me while I was a student in the Humanities Center at the Johns Hopkins University. Jonathan Galassi printed a selection of the translations in the *Paris Review* (Summer 1984); I thank him for his support and sustained encouragement. Gretchen Oberfranc provided much-needed editorial assistance in preparing the manuscript for publication. Finally, I would like to thank my friend Jörg Ruthel, with whom, many years ago, I first began these translations.

The work itself is dedicated to Laura.

In
the
Storm
of
Roses

Introduction: Poet on the Border

> I am not overly fond of poetry and don't
> read it willingly. In my reading, poems take
> up a very small space.
>
> Ingeborg Bachmann, in an interview
> with Alois Rummel, 1964

RARELY has a modern poet of serious rank been fêted so early or with such ceremony as was Ingeborg Bachmann. In 1953, the year her first volume of poetry was published, she received one of the most coveted literary prizes of postwar Germany from the "Gruppe 47." A year later the magazine *Der Spiegel* ran a cover story on the young Austrian poet, then living in Rome, which brought her to the attention of the general public. Two years later, with the publication of her second collection of poetry, public and critical acclaim redoubled. One of Germany's most noted critics and poets dedicated a chapter of his book on modern verse to Bachmann, explicitly establishing her rank and affiliation with poets such as Eliot, Rilke, and Gottfried Benn.[1] Three years later, in 1959, Bachmann was asked to give a series of lectures on modern poetics for a newly created chair at the University of Frankfurt, which prompted additional publicity, critical acclaim, and praise. A new star had risen, one of the most brightly burning in postwar Germany's literary heavens.

But this ascendence was undoubtedly one of Ingeborg Bachmann's greatest misfortunes. To be continually in the public eye, to have one's every gesture and word scrutinized, analyzed, publicly debated, was, for one as reticient and habitually taciturn as Bachmann, a painful embarrassment and a fetter on her work. Thrust into the role of celebrated poet,

---

[1] See Hans E. Holthusen, "Kämpfender Sprachgeist. Die Lyrik Ingeborg Bachmanns," in *Das Schöne und das Wahre*, Munich, 1958, pp. 246-76, one of the earliest and still most insightful treatments of Bachmann's poetry.

3

Bachmann wrote less and less poetry. Her second collection was her last; afterwards she published only a handful of individual poems, which, although among her finest and most powerful achievements, seemed to gravitate around the problem of silence or the impossibility of writing poetry. Many of them were dedicated to friends and fellow artists, as if the poems alone would not suffice but needed some external justification for their existence. In 1964, the year she received the Georg Büchner Prize, Bachmann published her last poem, which was also—like Hofmannsthal's Lord Chandos "Letter"—a farewell to poetry. It is entitled "No Delicacies" and begins:

> Nothing pleases me anymore.
>
> Should I
> dress a metaphor
> with an almond blossom?
> crucify syntax
> on a trick of light?
> Who will beat his brains
> over such superfluities—

And it concludes:

> Must I
> . . . .
> rip this paper apart,
> sweep away the plotted word operas,
> destroying thus: I you and he she it
>
> we you?
>
> (Still should. The others should.)
>
> My share, it should be dispersed.

If the slow dwindling into silence of Bachmann's poetic voice may be considered among the most fundamental and urgent questions her poetry raises, it should not be allowed to obscure the importance of her later contributions to other genres and disciplines. For if her uniquely probing voice, at once moral and philosophical, ultimately effaces itself from poetry, it makes itself plainly audible in more public realms: at the University of Frankfurt in a series of lectures on modern European literature entitled "Problems of Contemporary Poetry"; in radio plays such as *The Good God of Manhattan* (1958); in the short-story collections *The Thirtieth Year* (1961) and *Simultaneous* (1972); in the libretti for Hans Werner Henze's operas *The Prince of Homburg* (1960) and *The Young Lord* (1965); and in her first novel, *Malina* (1971), a complex, challenging work that nonetheless became a bestseller in Germany within a year of its publication. Intended as the first part of a trilogy called *Todesarten* (*Ways of Dying*), the novel might have become Bachmann's most extensive, successful continuation of problems first raised in her poetry, a vast fresco of contemporary Viennese society in the manner of Balzac or Joseph Roth, a philosophical meditation on the questions of gender, homeland, and borders. But on 26 September 1973 Bachmann's writing came to a halt when a fire broke out in her apartment. She died on October 17 from burns sustained in the accident, having suffered what a friend termed "the most terrible of *Todesarten*." She was forty-seven.

INGEBORG BACHMANN was born in 1926 in Klagenfurt, a small Austrian city near the Yugoslavian and Italian borders. As she recalls in an autobiographical note (see Appendix):

> I grew up in Carinthia, near the border, in a valley that has two names—a German one and a Slovenian one. And the house inhabited for generations by my ancestors—Austrians and Wends—still bears a foreign-sounding name. So near the border is yet an-

> other border: the border of language. I felt at home here and on the other side, with the tales of good and evil spirits from two or three countries. For behind the mountains, just an hour away, is Italy.

This remembrance is more than an allusion to the importance that foreign countries, and particularly Italy, would assume in her own life; it is also an acknowledgment of her multilingual Austrian heritage. For like Rilke, Hofmannsthal, Kafka, Freud, Wittgenstein, Canetti, and others, Bachmann lived in an environment of extreme racial, linguistic, and cultural diversity, in a country where the problem of borders posed itself with unusual urgency. These authors wrote in German, but often in regions where German was not the dominant language, or in places where the presence of racial and linguistic groups radically different from their own forced upon them the consciousness of the limits of their own language-world. They wrote what might be termed a "minority" German (which must not be confused with regionalism or dialect): a subtle, ironic, nuanced language different from the High German of northern Germany. Averse to dogmatic or sweeping generalizations (what the Austrians would term *Phrasen*), musical and yet clear-headed, rarely mystical and yet not without a trace of the uncanny—this language is also "Austria," the landscape that, if anywhere, Bachmann can call home.

In an interview in 1955 Bachmann insisted on the centrality of the Austrian heritage in her writing:

> It appears to me that Austria's particularity (which shouldn't be thought of in geographical categories, for its borders are not geographical) has been quite neglected. Poets like Grillparzer, Hofmannsthal, Rilke, and Robert Musil could never have been German. The Austrians have participated in so many cultures and thus developed a sense of the world which is different from that of the Germans.

This explains their sublime serenity, but also their sadness and many uncanny characteristics.[2]

And yet Bachmann states unequivocally, much as Kafka did in his diaries a generation earlier, that "all provincial and regional literary products are and will be sentenced to death." Even for the Austrian writer who feels at home in his tradition there can be only "German literature" (Interview, p. 12). Austria is now a fragment of its former empire, itself a living border, as Bachmann phrased it, "between a long, noble tradition and a gloomy future." Thus modern Austrian writers confront at least two borders: the linguistic border with High German, which forces them into a position of linguistic "excentricity," and the historical border with the now legally defunct Hapsburg Empire, which severs them from the homeland of their past. Not surprisingly, Bachmann conceives of the poet as writing in a state of permanent exile, legally homeless; her poem "Exile" begins: "I am a dead man who wanders / registered nowhere / unknown in the realm of the prefect . . . written off long ago." The poet's only home must be built from vowels, images, rhythms—from the poet's language:

> I with the German language
> this cloud about me
> that I keep as a house
> drive through all languages

What is the language Bachmann speaks? What is the script of the poetic utopia she inhabits, its rivers, coastlines, mountain ranges—its borders?

---

[2] This quotation is taken from the informative volume *Ingeborg Bachmann. Wir müssen wahre Sätze finden*, Munich, 1983, a collection of Bachmann's conversations and interviews, edited by Christine Koschel and Inge von Weidenbaum. Henceforth cited as Interview. All translations are my own.

WHAT MOST SURPRISED German audiences when Bachmann's poetry first appeared was that it did not sound like any of the major poetry of the previous generation of poets. Although occasional hints of Hofmannsthal, Trakl, or Brecht could be detected, especially in the first collection, readers generally agreed with Günter Blöcker's assertion that she had created her own categories.[3] Part of this originality was her characteristic fusion of abstract language with powerfully concrete images, or what was termed a "philosophical language of images." In her poems the temporal mode always seems on the verge of dissolving into the spatial, whereas a precise spatial image often stands for a temporal or philosophical abstraction. This tendency is evident in the opening poem of her first collection, in which the poetic "I" sails out into uncharted waters of experience, leaving behind the known borders of land, the small fishing hut, the sandbanks, and a lone tree on the cliffs. In the second stanza the poet addresses him or herself:[4]

> The dark water, thousand-eyed,
> opens its lashes of white foam

[3] Günter Blöcker, "Die gestundete Zeit," in *Ingeborg Bachmann. Eine Einführung*, Munich, 1968, pp. 22-25.

[4] The question of the gender of Ingeborg Bachmann's poetic voice, although not raised to the explicit level of reflection it attains in her later prose (especially *Malina*), still underlies many of the poems. Almost always the loved one addressed by the poet is female, which has led some feminist critics to speak of a "lesbian aesthetics." But the identification of Bachmann with the poetic voice in her poems needs some critical scrutiny. Bachmann's own most important statement on the subject can be found in a 1971 interview in which she speaks of the mixed gender of the narrator in *Malina*: "One of my oldest memories . . . is that I can narrate only from a masculine position. But I have often asked myself: why is that? I didn't understand, not even in my short stories, why I had to adopt the masculine 'I' so often. [In writing *Malina*] it was as if I had found my own person, that is, had not denied this feminine 'I' and still placed emphasis on the masculine 'I' " (Interview, pp. 99-100). In the present context, the poet will generally be referred to as female, a pragmatic decision that should not be interpreted as a resolution of the problem.

> to gaze at you, wide and long,
> thirty days long.

Here the temporal adjective "long" applies to the seeing waves, so that a month's journey, the poet's journey, is concretized with the image of an aquatic face. Water uncannily comes to life and is subjected to human laws of time. Sea and time merge threateningly midway through the poem when water monsters are used to symbolize the empty flow of human life:

> Blowing into conches the monsters of the sea glide
> onto the backs of the waves, they ride and strike
> the days into pieces with bared sabers; a red trace
> hangs in the water, sleep puts you there,
> on the rest of your hours,
> and your senses forsake you.

The threat is met with the poem's concluding evocation of a "sun shore, the sun shore that always returns." Against the dark flow of water and mortal time, against the land left behind with its storm-damaged tree, is posited the image of a sunlit utopia, which endlessly materializes and yet is still unreached.

A similar, though grimmer, version of departure is provided by the title poem of the collection *Mortgaged Time*: "Harder days are coming. / The mortgaged time, revocable at any hour, / takes shape on the horizon." Again time materializes into a threatening form, and the poet must leave behind lover, the light of flowers, the fish intestines "grown cold in the wind." This time the command is issued without the comfort of a utopic *telos*:

> Don't look round.
> Lace up your shoe.
> Drive back the hounds.

> Throw the fish in the sea.
> Blow out the lupines!
>
> Harder days are coming.

Another powerful objectification of time is realized in the title poem of Bachmann's second collection, *Invocation of the Great Bear*. The title refers to the constellation Ursa Major, that great bear in the sky made of shimmering stars:

> Great Bear, come down, shaggy night,
> cloud-coated beast with the old eyes,
> star eyes.
> Through the thickets your paws break
> shimmering with their claws,
> star claws.

This image of a mythic, galactic time evokes the poet's own mortality and is perceived as a threat, in this case as a wild animal. The bear plays with human worlds as with pine cones and orders a ritual feast of sacrifice. The final image is that of the beginning of history, the fall out of heaven into sin and human time. Christian angels are germanized into the fir trees of the North, "the great, winged ones / hurled down from Paradise."

Bachmann's "philosophical language of images," as well as her poetic meditation on the problem of time, were fostered by her study of philosophy. After the war, Bachmann began studying philosophy and law in Innsbruck and Graz, later moving to still-occupied Vienna and devoting herself to philosophy, psychology, and German literature. There she wrote a dissertation entitled *The Critical Reception of Martin Heidegger's Existential Philosophy* under the supervision of Victor Kraft, a follower of Moritz Schlick and Rudolf Carnap of the "Vienna Circle." Recalling the influence of this type of analytical philosophy on her own thinking, Bachmann characteristically stressed its "Austrian" rationality: "Another influence was exceedingly important for me: the Vienna School. In Vienna we have always waged a fierce battle against German metaphysics: down with German metaphysics which is our misfortune!" (Interview, p. 136).

So it was in the spirit of antagonism that the precocious twenty-two-year-old Austrian approached the author of *Being and Time*, to her the most metaphysical and "irrational" of modern German thinkers. Bachmann herself explains that her thesis was openly critical of Heidegger; she hoped, naively, that she would "topple" his German metaphysical system:

> Yes, I always say in reference to my thesis that it was written against Heidegger. For then I thought, at the age of twenty-two, that I would topple this man . . . Of course the Vienna logicians, Carnap and others, had tried to reduce Heidegger *ad absurdum*, although Heidegger of course was not even concerned with their formulation of the problem. (Interview, p. 137)

Bachmann naturally did not succeed in toppling Heidegger. Ironically, he was one of the few people, she claims, to have read her thesis. And strangely enough, for his seventieth birthday he asked his publishers for a *Festschrift* containing a poem by Bachmann and one by Paul Celan. "We both said no," Bachmann relates, "for I've read Heidegger's rectorial address [delivered at the University of Freiburg in 1933 and openly pro-Nazi], and even if this speech didn't exist there would still be something [objectionable] in his work. We are always in danger of being seduced by German irrationalism" (Interview, p. 137).

The philosopher who, Bachmann freely admits, influenced her was her Viennese contemporary Ludwig Wittgenstein:

> I wouldn't call it a direct influence, for the gap between philosophy and writing is too large. But what

I really learned, and this is why I speak of an influence, was an incredibly precise mode of thinking and clear expression. (Interview, p. 136)

His *Tractatus* and *Philosophical Investigations* were almost unknown in German-speaking countries after the war, and Bachmann helped convince the Suhrkamp Verlag to republish them in an accessible edition. In 1953, the same year her first collection of poetry appeared, she wrote one of the earliest German critical essays on Wittgenstein's thought: "Ludwig Wittgenstein: A Chapter in the Recent History of German Philosophy."[5] Bachmann never conceived of philosophy and poetry as mutually exclusive enterprises. Like her fellow Austrians Hermann Broch and Robert Musil, she employed both the language of science—logical, mathematical, precise—and the "language of the soul" in her writings. Her ethical concern required both.

Bachmann clearly saw Wittgenstein's philosophical project as parallel to her own in poetry. In her essay of 1953 she singled out Wittgenstein's confrontation with the limits—or borders—of language:

> What merits our renewed and endlessly renewable consideration are not [Wittgenstein's] clarifying, negative propositions, which limit philosophy to a logical analysis of scientific language and restrict the analysis of the real world to specialized scientific fields; but rather *his despairing attempt to chart the limits of linguistic expression*, which provides the *Tractatus* with its inner tension, a tension into which he eventually disappears.[6]

[5] First published in *Frankfurter Hefte. Zeitschrift für Kultur und Politik*, July 1953.
[6] Taken from *Ingeborg Bachmann. Werke*, ed. Christine Koschel, Inge von Weidenbaum, and Clemens Münster, Munich, 1978, vol. 4, p. 13 (my emphasis).

Wittgenstein's attention to the limits of language corresponds to Bachmann's own view that "we stand, think, and speak on this side of the 'borders.' The feeling of the world as a bordered fragment arises because we ourselves, as metaphysical subjects, are no longer parts of the world but rather 'borders' " (*Werke*, vol. 4, p. 20). The same thought finds expression in one of Bachmann's last poems, "Bohemia Lies by the Sea," itself a re-working of Shakespeare's affirmation in *The Winter's Tale* that the "deserts of Bohemia" could be reached by ship:[7]

> I border still on a word and on a different land,
> I border, like little else, on everything more and more,
>
> a man from Bohemia, a vagrant, a player
> who holds nothing and whom nothing holds,
> granted only, by a questionable sea, to gaze at the
>   land of my choice.

These lines might be considered one of Bachmann's most emblematic statements on the function of the poet: as a bridge or border to utopia, both land and language, an imaginative "nowhere" where possibility abides rather than necessity, and the speaking subject is free.

IN 1953 BACHMANN moved to Italy, voluntarily exiling herself from her native Austria. Her discovery of the Mediterranean landscape profoundly influenced her poetry and prose alike, as portrayed in a poem of her second collection entitled "The Firstborn Land." It begins:

> To my firstborn land, to the South
> I went—and found, naked and poor,

---

[7] *The Winter's Tale*, III, iii: "Thou art perfect then our ship hath touched upon / The deserts of Bohemia?" Bachmann reverses Shakespeare's negative formulation of the "desert" Bohemia, appropriating it for her utopic conception of "Austria."

and up to their waist in the sea,
city and castle.

At first the poet is blind, and the skeleton of a tree hanging over her offers no dream. "No rosemary blooms there, / no bird refreshes / its song in the fountain." But the poison of a viper makes the poet close her eyes, paradoxically preparing for the awakening of vision:

And as I drank myself,
and the earthquakes rocked
my firstborn land,
my eyes awoke.

Life fell down to me.

There the stone isn't dead.
The wick flies up
when a glance sets it alight.

Life "falls down" to the poet in the south, in "Italy," which like Austria must be understood as more than a geographical space, as the landscape of Dante, Petrarch, and Ungaretti, as the mouth of a cave leading back to classical Rome, the catacombs of the early Christians, and the eruptions of Vesuvius. An example of her understanding of this landscape is the essay "What I Saw and Heard in Rome" (included in the present collection), in which the stones of the ancient city are brought to speak of their complex, layered past.

Paradoxically, in Italy Bachmann is not "in exile." To Kuno Räber she remarked: "Now I am *residente* and have my permanent home in Rome; nothing can happen to me anymore."[8] And in a statement prepared for a Vienna radio station, she

---

[8] "Erinnerung an Ingeborg Bachmann," *Süddeutsche Zeitung*, 12 October 1974.

explained: "I have never been able to explain why I moved to Rome. The city has something natural in it for me . . . [for] I grew up on the Italian border and heard Italian spoken at home." While writing in German (the "cloud" she keeps around her like a house) in her Rome apartment, Bachmann is in two places at once, leads a doubled existence: "From the moment I enter my study I am in Vienna, not Rome." This doubleness grants her not only the necessary distance for her work but also an intensified, focused vision of her life in Austria: "I am more in Vienna because I am in Rome, for without this distance I couldn't imagine writing" (Interview, p. 65).

Bachmann's second collection of poems was published in 1956, three years after her move to Italy, and clearly reflects in images and form this change in her environment. Critics have generally concurred that it marks a strengthening of her poetic voice. The images are calmer and yet more powerfully direct. She makes frequent use of rhyme and measured verse, adopting, as one critic put it, a classicism that merges with the oldest images and archetypes of Western literature.[9] Or, as Bachmann phrased it in her essay on Rome, referring to the three cypress trees reflected on the glass façade of the railway station, engraved in an unmistakable script: "The classical form is the simplest, and old and new texts represent it equally well."

What gives an inner tension to this collection is the persistent juxtaposition and rivalry between a Germanic, wooded, snow-filled landscape and a vibrant Mediterranean seascape of light, artistic beauty, vision, and "life." The temporal movement of the collection is also a migration from North to South, from the initial, justly celebrated poems "Invocation of the Great Bear," "My Bird," and "Land of Fog" to the equally fine hymn of praise "To the Sun" and the concluding poem cycle "Songs of Flight." "Land of Fog" presents Bachmann's most extreme vision of a mythopoeic North, all the more bar-

---

[9] See Holthusen, "Kämpfender Sprachgeist."

ren and chill because it is perceived through the eyes of the jealous, abandoned lover;

> In winter my love
> is among the beasts of the forest.
> The vixen knows
> I must be back before morning
> and she laughs.
> How the clouds tremble! And a layer
> of brittle ice falls
> on my snow-collar.

"Faithless is my love," the poet laments, concluding with the bitter condemnation of her past: "It is fog land I have seen, / fog heart I have eaten." Simple, direct, classical, this poem derives part of its force by echoing the biblical cadence and theme of the Song of Songs,[10] although the latter's content has been ironically reversed. The communion with nature, the interchangeability of human, animal, and plant forms posited in Solomon's "High Song" is in Bachmann's version granted only to the faithless lover, not to the jealous speaker who stands alone on the riverbank.

Yet it would be wrong to assume that the poles of North and South can be equated in Bachmann's poetry with a beautiful, vital present and an evil past. A more just metaphor would be the positive and negative points of a battery, both of which are needed to generate a current of poetic energy. In *Invocation of the Great Bear*, Bachmann exploits her myth of North and South and the contrasting associations they provide, just as earlier she had relied on the contrast between land and water, the rivers and the banks between which they flow. But she spe-

---

[10] "I am a rose of Sharon, a lily of the valleys. As a lily among brambles, so is my love among maidens. . . ." Song of Solomon, chap. 2, v. 1-2. This book also seems to have influenced portions of "Songs of Flight," just as generally Bachmann's language reflects her sustained readings of the Old and New Testaments.

cifically rejects the notion of a successful "escape" to the South, be it the German Romantics' conception of Italy or the "pilgrimages" of contemporary Northern tourists in search of sun and exotic landscapes. Already in the early poem "Autumn Maneuver" she had poked fun at the latter in the ironic lines:

> Let us take a journey! Let us see sunsets under
>   cypresses
> or palm trees, or in orange groves,
> at reduced prices, sunsets
> that have no equal!

And she affirms in the opening stanza of the same poem that "flight to the South, where the birds fly, won't help us."

Thus Bachmann's use of light imagery is not as categorically affirmative as it might appear. The "South" opens the poet's eyes, introduces her to beauty, gives her "life." But this same process exposes her to the inevitable danger of blindness. Again in "Autumn Maneuver" we read the characteristic lines: "and sometimes / a splinter of dream-filled marble hits me / where I am vulnerable, through beauty, in the eye." The experience of classical antiquity, the beauty of a marble column, is also one of pain, which ultimately intercedes between poet and world, closing off the poet's sight. The same thought is formulated in the concluding lines of "To the Sun," which begins as an unconditional hymn of praise to the sun's beauty, virtues, even miracles, but finishes thus: "Hence not for the moon or the stars . . . / But for your sake and soon endlessly and as if nothing else mattered / I shall lament the unavoidable loss of my eyes." The light of beauty does not result in *Aufklärung* or illumination, but in darkness.

For the Southern landscape is also marked by unrequited love and the pain of jealousy. Bachmann's fine poem cycle "Songs of Flight" is preceded by the ominous stanza from Petrarch's *Trionfi*: "Dura legge d'Amor! ma, ben che obliqua, /

Servar convensi." The law of Love is severe, even obscure, but we must serve it. The German title "Lieder *auf* der Flucht," literally "Songs [written] *while* in Flight," makes more explicit than English usage will allow that the poet is still denied a homeland. Here North and South meet; the exotic Mediterranean landscape of palm trees and oranges is immobilized by snow and ice:

> The palm frond breaks in snow,
> the stairs are falling in.
> The city lies stiff and gleams
> in a strange winter glow.
> . . . .
> The rich winter tinsel,
> the mandarin gold,
> whirls in the wild squalls.
> The blood orange rolls.

Later the depiction of human love becomes a communion with this Mediterranean territory, a remarkably sensuous merging of poet and world:

> Within, your breast is a sea
> that pulls me to its bed.
> Within, your hip is a landing pier
> for my ships, coming home
> from too long a voyage.
> . . . .
> Within, your flesh is melon light,
> sweet and delicious unendingly.

But inevitably this union results in the pain of separation: "You want the summer lightning, and fling the knives . . . / and finally you sense how love expires." Now the sun does not warm, the sea is voiceless. The dead have not been released from their snow-locked graves. "Release me," the poet implores, "I cannot die any longer."

It is song, after the poet's death, that melts the winter of the Mediterranean:

> Wait for my death and then hear me again.
> The snow basket tips over and the water sings,
> all sounds merge into the Toledo, the ice is thawing.
> . . . .
> Syllables in oleander,
> word in acacian green,
> cascades from the wall.

In the final stanzas of the cycle, Petrarch's notion of the triumph of love is re-stated: "Love has a triumph and death has one, the time and the time thereafter." But we have none: "Only the sinking of stars about us. Reflected splendor and silence." Then Bachmann concludes, echoing Rilke,[11] with lines that might well be placed as an epitaph to all her work: "Yet the song above the dust / one day will rise above us."

THE POEMS written after "Songs of Flight," though unmistakably from Bachmann's hand, read as if the poet had reached a higher, more sovereign, and yet more painful plateau of consciousness. The clipped Austrian accent is there, the same rhythm and lightly atonal musicality, the lamenting, never self-pitying voice. And yet an inner certainty is missing. The poems are luminous, but suffused with a light that knows itself close to extinction. As noted previously, these are essentially poems about poems, or rather, poems about the impossibility of writing poetry. Bachmann continually confronts the problem of the poet's "dying words," her last poem, denying what she feels is imminent:

---

[11] See the conclusion to Rilke's nineteenth sonnet in the first part of his *Sonnets to Orpheus*: "Einzig das Lied überm Land / heiligt und feiert" ("Only the song above the land / sanctifies and celebrates").

> And above all not this: the image
> in the web of dust, hollow roll
> of syllables, last words.
>
> No dying word,
> you words!

Her poem "Enigma," dedicated to the man who, years earlier in Italy, had set her poetry to music, is dark and resigned;

> Nothing more will come.
> Spring will never be again.
> . . . .
> You shouldn't cry,
> the music says.
>
> Otherwise
> no one
> says
> anything.

Of course, Bachmann also wrote "Bohemia Lies by the Sea," arguably one of her best poems, which reaffirms the same belief in a coming utopia that had so strongly informed her earlier work and, perhaps, had permitted her to stay the sentence of silence. But then she did write her last poem, did articulate the wish for self-obliteration in the last line of "No Delicacies": "My share, it should be dispersed." In her acceptance speech for the Georg Büchner Prize, Christa Wolf quoted Bachmann's last poem, commenting:

> This is language on the other side of belief, but language nevertheless. Metaphors are rejected by a metaphor; the lines that renounce first-rate morsels of words are themselves first-rate. The poem that disowns art must paradoxically be a work of

art. . . . The poet who expresses herself completely does not cancel herself out: the wish for obliteration remains as a witness. Her share will not be dispersed.[12]

Why did Bachmann stop writing poetry? The question is too complex to be answered in the present context. Bachmann herself tended to be evasive in responding to the question, which her readers never tired of asking. Perhaps the more important question is not why she stopped writing poetry but why she moved from poetry to other genres. For Bachmann never stopped writing. As Christa Wolf has pointed out, not only does her poetry continue to speak long after the poet has voiced the wish for self-obliteration; but Bachmann also began to write works for a wider audience—works less hermetic, more widely read, more effective in a social and political sense. Many of the poems in *Mortgaged Time* had a Brechtian ring in their critique of Germany's Nazi past. But they were articulated in a "grand style," their perspective (as in the sparse but somewhat ponderous "Message") was that of *Weltgeschichte*. Bachmann's last poems seem to issue from the personal grief caused not by the crimes of German leaders but by the suffering of the nameless. In "No Delicacies" the poet confesses:

---

[12] The title of Christa Wolf's acceptance speech ("Should I dress a metaphor with an almond blossom?") is taken from Bachmann's last poem, "No Delicacies." The speech was reprinted in an English translation, in *New German Critique*, no. 23, Spring / Summer 1981. This poem may not actually be Bachmann's last. Several others, including "Enigma" and "Truly," may have been written after "No Delicacies," although "Truly" is based on an earlier, unpublished poem entitled "On the Way to Prague." However, Wolf's comments, as well as my own about the problem of silence, are valid no matter what the last poem is. Although Bachmann undoubtedly attempted to write after "No Delicacies," this poem reads as if nothing else could follow—which is apparently why her editors placed it at the end of her collected poems.

> I have learned to be considerate
> with the words
> that exist
> (for the lowest class)
>
>   hunger
>   disgrace
>   tears
> and
>   darkness

If Bachmann's "silence" is to be understood at all, it must be seen against the ground of her peculiarly Austrian moral consciousness, her concern with the right words for "the lowest class." Like her fellow Austrian Hofmannsthal, whose Lord Chandos "Letter" expressed moral as well as metaphysical despair and who abandoned poetry for the more social genre of drama, Bachmann was increasingly concerned with the fate of the unnamed, the homeless, the ordinary victims of oppression, and often took part in the left-wing protest movements of the period. She believed that war never really ends but is waged in private circumstances. And so writing came to be a kind of antidote to reality, a gesture of exposure and condemnation, a statement "against the continuing terror." For "we don't really die of diseases," she insisted, "we die as a result of what has been done to us" (Interview, p. 110).

Bachmann's voice, the "human voice" praised by the politically committed Christa Wolf, did not die out with her last poem. It changed tack, field, and register, but it is clearly the same voice. We hear it, for instance, in the refrain that runs through her last novel, *Malina*, lamenting the crime and suffering of the present, crying out, against all odds, for the creation of what she came to define as "utopia":

> A day will come when all people have black-golden eyes, they will see beauty and be released from filth

and every burden, they will lift themselves into the air, walk beneath the waters, forget their callouses and afflictions. A day will come, they will be free, all people will be free, even from the kind of freedom they have imagined. A greater freedom will come to be, it will exceed all measure, it will be for a whole life. . . .

These words are the last steps of a long journey, a journey that began twenty years earlier in the poems presented here.

FROM THE COLLECTION

Mortgaged Time

Ausfahrt

Vom Lande steigt Rauch auf.
Die kleine Fischerhütte behalt im Aug,
denn die Sonne wird sinken,
ehe du zehn Meilen zurückgelegt hast.

Das dunkle Wasser, tausendäugig,
schlägt die Wimper von weißer Gischt auf,
um dich anzusehen, groß und lang,
dreißig Tage lang.

Auch wenn das Schiff hart stampft
und einen unsicheren Schritt tut,
steh ruhig auf Deck.

An den Tischen essen sie jetzt
den geräucherten Fisch;
dann werden die Männer hinknien
und die Netze flicken,
aber nachts wird geschlafen,
eine Stunde oder zwei Stunden,
und ihre Hände werden weich sein,
frei von Salz und Öl,
weich wie das Brot des Traumes,
von dem sie brechen.

Die erste Welle der Nacht schlägt ans Ufer,
die zweite erreicht schon dich.
Aber wenn du scharf hinüberschaust,
kannst du den Baum noch sehen,
der trotzig den Arm hebt
– einen hat ihm der Wind schon abgeschlagen
– und du denkst: wie lange noch,
wie lange noch

Leaving Port

Smoke rises off the land.
Keep your eye on the small fishing hut,
for the sun will sink
before you've put ten miles behind you.

The dark water, thousand-eyed,
opens its lashes of white foam
to gaze at you, wide and long,
thirty days long.

Even when the ship pitches hard
and takes a faltering step,
stay calm on deck.

At the tables now they're eating
smoked fish;
then the men will kneel down
and start mending the nets.
But at night they sleep,
an hour or two,
and their hands will grow soft,
free from salt and oil,
as soft as the dream bread
they break.

The first wave of night rolls onto the shore,
the second has already reached you.
But if you look closely over there
you can still see the tree
holding up a defiant arm
—the wind has already knocked one down
—and you think to yourself: how much longer,
how much longer

wird das krumme Holz den Wettern standhalten?
Vom Land ist nichts mehr zu sehen.
Du hättest dich mit einer Hand in die Sandbank krallen
oder mit einer Locke an die Klippen heften sollen.

In die Muscheln blasend, gleiten die Ungeheuer des Meers
auf die Rücken der Wellen, sie reiten und schlagen
mit blanken Säbeln die Tage in Stücke, eine rote Spur
bleibt im Wasser, dort legt dich der Schlaf hin,
auf den Rest deiner Stunden,
und dir schwinden die Sinne.

Da ist etwas mit den Tauen geschehen,
man ruft dich, und du bist froh,
daß man dich braucht. Das Beste
ist die Arbeit auf den Schiffen,
die weithin fahren,
das Tauknüpfen, das Wasserschöpfen,
das Wändedichten und das Hüten der Fracht.
Das Beste ist, müde zu sein und am Abend
hinzufallen. Das Beste ist, am Morgen,
mit dem ersten Licht, hell zu werden,
gegen den unverrückbaren Himmel zu stehen,
der ungangbaren Wasser nicht zu achten
und das Schiff über die Wellen zu heben,
auf das immerwiederkehrende Sonnenufer zu.

will that twisted wood hold out against the storms?
There is nothing left of the land.
You should have clawed into the sandbank with your hand
or pinned yourself to the cliffs with a lock of hair.

Blowing into conches the monsters of the sea glide
onto the backs of the waves, they ride and strike
the days into pieces with bared sabers; a red trace
hangs in the water, sleep puts you there,
on the rest of your hours,
and your senses forsake you.

Now something's wrong with the rigging,
they call you and you're glad
to be needed. The best thing
on ships that travel far
is the work—
knotting ropes and bailing out water,
sealing walls and guarding the freight.
The best thing is to be tired and, in the evening,
to fall into bed. The best thing is, in the morning,
to rise with the first light,
standing against an immovable sky,
paying no heed to impassable waters,
raising your ship over the waves
toward the sun shore,
the sun shore that always returns.

Abschied von England

Ich habe deinen Boden kaum betreten,
schweigsames Land, kaum einen Stein berührt,
ich war von deinem Himmel so hoch gehoben,
so in Wolken, Dunst und in noch Ferneres gestellt,
daß ich dich schon verließ,
als ich vor Anker ging.

Du hast meine Augen geschlossen
mit Meerhauch und Eichenblatt,
von meinen Tränen begossen,
hieltst du die Gräser satt;
aus meinen Träumen gelöst,
wagten sich Sonnen heran,
doch alles war wieder fort,
wenn dein Tag begann.
Alles blieb ungesagt.

Durch die Straßen flatterten die großen grauen Vögel
und wiesen mich aus.
War ich je hier?

Ich wollte nicht gesehen werden.

Meine Augen sind offen.
Meerhauch und Eichenblatt?
Unter den Schlangen des Meers
seh ich, an deiner Statt,
das Land meiner Seele erliegen.

Ich habe seinen Boden nie betreten.

Departure from England

I have scarcely trod your soil,
silent land, scarcely touched a stone.
Your sky had lifted me so high,
placed me so in clouds, mist and beyond
that I left you
when I cast anchor.

You shut my eyes
with sea breeze and oak leaf;
watered with my tears,
you kept the grasses sated;
freed from my dreams,
suns dared to approach.
Yet everything was gone again
when your day began.
Everything remained unsaid.

Great gray birds fluttered through the streets
and banished me.
Was I ever here?

I did not want to be seen.

My eyes are open.
Sea breeze and oak leaf?
Beneath the snakes of the ocean
I see, in your stead,
the land of my soul succumb.

I have never trod her soil.

Fall ab, Herz

Fall ab, Herz, vom Baum der Zeit,
fallt, ihr Blätter, aus den erkalteten Ästen,
die einst die Sonne umarmt',
fallt, wie Tränen fallen aus dem geweiteten Aug!

Fliegt noch die Locke taglang im Wind
um des Landgotts gebräunte Stirn,
unter dem Hemd preßt die Faust
schon die klaffende Wunde.

Drum sei hart, wenn der zarte Rücken der Wolken
sich dir einmal noch beugt,
nimm es für nichts, wenn der Hymettos die Waben
noch einmal dir füllt.

Denn wenig gilt dem Landmann ein Halm in der Dürre,
wenig ein Sommer vor unserem großen Geschlecht.

Und was bezeugt schon dein Herz?
Zwischen gestern und morgen schwingt es,
lautlos und fremd,
und was es schlägt,
ist schon sein Fall aus der Zeit.

Fall, My Heart

Fall, my heart, from the tree of time,
fall, you leaves, from icy branches
that once the sun embraced,
fall, as tears fall from the widened eye!

For days the earth god's hair blows in the wind
about his sun-worn brow,
while his fist clenches
the gaping wound beneath his shirt.

So be hard when the tender back of a cloud
bows down to you once more.
Pay no heed to the Hymettus bee,
should he fill your honeycomb again.

For a straw in times of drought means little to the peasant,
a summer little to our great lineage.

And to what can your heart attest?
Between yesterday and tomorrow it swings,
foreign and mute,
and what it beats,
is its fall out of time.

Dunkles zu sagen

Wie Orpheus spiel ich
auf den Saiten des Lebens den Tod
und in die Schönheit der Erde
und deiner Augen, die den Himmel verwalten,
weiß ich nur Dunkles zu sagen.

Vergiß nicht, daß auch du, plötzlich,
an jenem Morgen, als dein Lager
noch naß war von Tau und die Nelke
an deinem Herzen schlief,
den dunklen Fluß sahst,
der an dir vorbeizog.

Die Saite des Schweigens
gespannt auf die Welle von Blut,
griff ich dein tönendes Herz.
Verwandelt ward deine Locke
ins Schattenhaar der Nacht,
der Finsternis schwarze Flocken
beschneiten dein Antlitz.

Und ich gehör dir nicht zu.
Beide klagen wir nun.

Aber wie Orpheus weiß ich
auf der Seite des Todes das Leben,
und mir blaut
dein für immer geschlossenes Aug.

Dark Words

Like Orpheus I play
death on the strings of life.
And in the face of the earth's beauty
and your eyes, that govern the heavens,
I have only dark words to say.

Don't forget that one morning,
when your camp was still wet
with dew and the carnation
slept by your heart,
you also saw the dark river
dart past.

Its string of silence
stretched taut on a wave of blood,
I plucked your sounding heart.
Your hair was changed
into shadow locks of night,
black flakes of darkness
snowed down on your face.

And I don't belong to you.
Now we are both lamenting.

But like Orpheus I know of
life on the side of death.
And blue before me
I see your eye, forever closed.

Paris

Aufs Rad der Nacht geflochten
schlafen die Verlorenen
in den donnernden Gängen unten,
doch wo wir sind, ist Licht.

Wir haben die Arme voll Blumen,
Mimosen aus vielen Jahren;
Goldnes fällt von Brücke zu Brücke
atemlos in den Fluß.

Kalt ist das Licht,
noch kälter der Stein vor dem Tor,
und die Schalen der Brunnen
sind schon zur Hälfte geleert.

Was wird sein, wenn wir, vom Heimweh
benommen bis ans fliehende Haar,
hier bleiben und fragen: was wird sein,
wenn wir die Schönheit bestehen?

Auf den Wagen des Lichts gehoben,
wachend auch, sind wir verloren,
auf den Straßen der Genien oben,
doch wo wir nicht sind, ist Nacht.

Paris

Lashed to the wheel of night,
the lost ones sleep
down below, in the thundering tunnels—
but where we are, there is light.

Our arms are laden with flowers,
mimosa from many years.
Gold falls from bridge to bridge,
breathless in the river.

Cold is the light,
colder still the stone before the gate;
and all the fountain basins
are half drained.

What will happen if we stay here,
homesick to the root of our flowing hair,
and ask: what will happen
if we survive beauty's trial?

Lifted high on the wagon of light,
though waking, we are lost
in the streets of genius, above—
but where we are not, there is night.

Die große Fracht

Die große Fracht des Sommers ist verladen,
das Sonnenschiff im Hafen liegt bereit,
wenn hinter dir die Möwe stürzt und schreit.
Die große Fracht des Sommers ist verladen.

Das Sonnenschiff im Hafen liegt bereit,
und auf die Lippen der Galionsfiguren
tritt unverhüllt das Lächeln der Lemuren.
Das Sonnenschiff im Hafen liegt bereit.

Wenn hinter dir die Möwe stürzt und schreit,
kommt aus dem Westen der Befehl zu sinken;
doch offnen Augs wirst du im Licht ertrinken,
wenn hinter dir die Möwe stürzt und schreit.

The Heavy Freight

The heavy freight of summer is on board,
waiting in the harbor the sun ship lies
when at your back the seagull swoops and cries.
The heavy freight of summer is on board.

Waiting in the harbor the sun ship lies,
and along the lips of figureheads
the cunning smile of lemurs threads.
Waiting in the harbor the sun ship lies.

When at your back the seagull swoops and cries
the order to sink comes eastward into sight.
Yet open-eyed you will drown in light
when at your back the seagull swoops and cries.

Herbstmanöver

Ich sage nicht: das war gestern. Mit wertlosem
Sommergeld in den Taschen liegen wir wieder
auf der Spreu des Hohns, im Herbstmanöver der Zeit.
Und der Fluchtweg nach Süden kommt uns nicht,
wie den Vögeln, zustatten. Vorüber, am Abend,
ziehen Fischkutter und Gondeln, und manchmal
trifft mich ein Splitter traumsatten Marmors,
wo ich verwundbar bin, durch Schönheit, im Aug.

In den Zeitungen lese ich viel von der Kälte
und ihren Folgen, von Törichten und Toten,
von Vertriebenen, Mördern und Myriaden
von Eisschollen, aber wenig, was mir behagt.
Warum auch? Vor dem Bettler, der mittags kommt,
schlag ich die Tür zu, denn es ist Frieden
und man kann sich den Anblick ersparen, aber nicht
im Regen das freudlose Sterben der Blätter.

Laßt uns eine Reise tun! Laßt uns unter Zypressen
oder auch unter Palmen oder in den Orangenhainen
zu verbilligten Preisen Sonnenuntergänge sehen,
die nicht ihresgleichen haben! Laßt uns die
unbeantworteten Briefe an das Gestern vergessen!
Die Zeit tut Wunder. Kommt sie uns aber unrecht,
mit dem Pochen der Schuld: wir sind nicht zu Hause.
Im Keller des Herzens, schlaflos, find ich mich wieder
auf der Spreu des Hohns, im Herbstmanöver der Zeit.

Autumn Maneuver

I don't say: that was before. Our pockets stuffed
with worthless summer money, we lie once more
on the chaff of scorn, in the autumn maneuver of time.
And flight to the South,
where the birds fly, won't help us. In the evening
fishing trawlers and gondolas glide past, and sometimes
a splinter of dream-filled marble hits me
where I am vulnerable, through beauty, in the eye.

In the newspapers I read much about the cold
and its consequences, about fools and the dead,
about the banished, the murderers and myriads
of ice-floes, but little that comforts me.
Should it be otherwise? At noon a beggar comes
and I slam the door in his face; for there is peace
and you can spare yourself an unpleasant sight, though not
the joyless dying of leaves when it rains.

Let us take a journey! Let us see sunsets under cypresses
or palm trees, or in orange groves,
at reduced prices, sunsets
that have no equal! Let us forget
our unanswered letters to yesterday!
Time works wonders. But should it come unjustly,
with the throb of guilt: we are not at home.
In the cellar of my heart, sleepless, I find myself once more
on the chaff of scorn, in the autumn maneuver of time.

Die gestundete Zeit

Es kommen härtere Tage.
Die auf Widerruf gestundete Zeit
wird sichtbar am Horizont.
Bald mußt du den Schuh schnüren
und die Hunde zurückjagen in die Marschhöfe.
Denn die Eingeweide der Fische
sind kalt geworden im Wind.
Ärmlich brennt das Licht der Lupinen.
Dein Blick spurt im Nebel:
die auf Widerruf gestundete Zeit
wird sichtbar am Horizont.

Drüben versinkt dir die Geliebte im Sand,
er steigt um ihr wehendes Haar,
er fällt ihr ins Wort,
er befiehlt ihr zu schweigen,
er findet sie sterblich
und willig dem Abschied
nach jeder Umarmung.

Sieh dich nicht um.
Schnür deinen Schuh.
Jag die Hunde zurück.
Wirf die Fische ins Meer.
Lösch die Lupinen!

Es kommen härtere Tage.

Mortgaged Time

Harder days are coming.
The mortgaged time,
revocable at any hour,
takes shape on the horizon.
Soon you must lace up your shoe
and chase the hounds back to the marsh farms.
For the fish entrails
have grown cold in the wind.
The lupins' light burns dimly.
Your gaze gropes in the fog:
the mortgaged time,
revocable at any hour,
takes shape on the horizon.

Over there your love sinks in the sand.
It climbs around her waving hair,
it breaks into her words,
it commands her to be still,
it finds her mortal
and willing to part
after every embrace.

Don't look round.
Lace up your shoe.
Chase back the hounds.
Throw the fish in the sea.
Blow out the lupins!

Harder days are coming.

Holz und Späne

Von den Hornissen will ich schweigen,
denn sie sind leicht zu erkennen.
Auch die laufenden Revolutionen
sind nicht gefährlich.
Der Tod im Gefolge des Lärms
ist beschlossen von jeher.

Doch vor den Eintagsfliegen und den Frauen
nimm dich in acht, vor den Sonntagsjägern,
den Kosmetikern, den Unentschiedenen, Wohlmeinenden,
von keiner Verachtung getroffnen.

Aus den Wäldern trugen wir Reisig und Stämme,
und die Sonne ging uns lange nicht auf.
Berauscht vom Papier am Fließband,
erkenn ich die Zweige nicht wieder,
noch das Moos, in dunkleren Tinten gegoren,
noch das Wort, in die Rinden geschnitten,
wahr und vermessen.

Blätterverschleiß, Spruchbänder,
schwarze Plakate ... Bei Tag und bei Nacht
bebt, unter diesen und jenen Sternen,
die Maschine des Glaubens. Aber ins Holz,
solang es noch grün ist, und mit der Galle,
solang sie noch bitter ist, bin ich
zu schreiben gewillt, was im Anfang war!

Seht zu, daß ihr wachbleibt!

Wood Chips

Of hornets I wish to be silent
for they're easy to recognize.
The current revolutions
aren't dangerous either.
Death in the retinue of noise
has been decided from the very first.

Yet of one-day flies and women
beware; and of Sunday hunters,
beauticians, the undecided, the well-meaning—
all the unstigmatized.

We emerged from the forest carrying brushwood and logs,
and the sun was long in rising.
Dizzied by the paper on assembly lines,
I no longer recognize the twigs—
nor the moss, fermented in darker inks,
nor the word, inscribed in bark,
true and arrogant.

Worn-out pages, banners,
black posters . . . By day and by night,
beneath this and that star,
the machine of belief is humming. But into the wood,
as long as it's green, and with bile,
as long as it's bitter, I intend
to write the word of the beginning!

Make sure you stay awake.

Der Spur der Späne, die flogen, folgt
der Hornissenschwarm, und am Brunnen
sträubt sich der Lockung,
die uns einst schwächte,
das Haar.

A swarm of hornets trails the chips
that flew from the axe; and at the fountain,
bristling against the temptation
that once weakened us,
is my hair.

Früher Mittag

Still grünt die Linde im eröffneten Sommer,
weit aus den Städten gerückt, flirrt
der mattglänzende Tagmond. Schon ist Mittag,
schon regt sich im Brunnen der Strahl,
schon hebt sich unter den Scherben
des Märchenvogels geschundener Flügel,
und die vom Steinwurf entstellte Hand
sinkt ins erwachende Korn.

Wo Deutschlands Himmel die Erde schwärzt,
sucht sein enthaupteter Engel ein Grab für den Haß
und reicht dir die Schüssel des Herzens.

Eine Handvoll Schmerz verliert sich über den Hügel.

Sieben Jahre später
fällt es dir wieder ein,
am Brunnen vor dem Tore,
blick nicht zu tief hinein,
die Augen gehen dir über.

Sieben Jahre später,
in einem Totenhaus,
trinken die Henker von gestern
den goldenen Becher aus.
Die Augen täten dir sinken.

Schon ist Mittag, in der Asche
krümmt sich das Eisen, auf den Dorn
ist die Fahne gehißt, und auf den Felsen
uralten Traums bleibt fortan
der Adler geschmiedet.

Early Noon

Softly the linden grows green in the opening summer.
Far from cities the dull gleaming moon
of day flickers. Already it is noon:
already the rays of light stir in the fountain,
already the battered wing of the fairytale bird
lifts itself from broken glass,
and the hand, deformed from throwing stones,
sinks into awakening corn.

Where Germany's sky blackens the earth
its beheaded angel seeks a grave for its hate
and hands you the bowl of its heart.

A handful of pain is lost over the hill.

Seven years later
you realize once more,
by the fountain in front of the gate:
don't look in too deep
for your eyes will swell with tears.

Seven years later,
in a house of death,
yesterday's hangmen drink
the golden goblet dry.
Your eyes would sink to the floor.

Already it is noon; the iron
grows crooked in the ashes, the flag
is raised on a thorn, and in the rocks
of an ancient dream the eagle
shall remain wrought.

Nur die Hoffnung kauert erblindet im Licht.

Lös ihr die Fessel, führ sie
die Halde herab, leg ihr
die Hand auf das Aug, daß sie
kein Schatten versengt!

Wo Deutschlands Erde den Himmel schwärzt,
sucht die Wolke nach Worten und füllt den Krater mit
    Schweigen,
eh sie der Sommer im schütteren Regen vernimmt.

Das Unsägliche geht, leise gesagt, übers Land:
schon ist Mittag.

Only hope cowers blinded in the light.

Take off hope's chains, lead her down
the slope, put your
hand over her eyes—
let no shadow scorch her!

Where Germany's earth blackens the sky,
a cloud looks for words and fills the crater with silence,
before summer hears its call through the thin rain.

The unspeakable, said softly, steals over the land:
already it is noon.

Alle Tage

Der Krieg wird nicht mehr erklärt,
sondern fortgesetzt. Das Unerhörte
ist alltäglich geworden. Der Held
bleibt den Kämpfen fern. Der Schwache
ist in die Feuerzonen gerückt.
Die Uniform des Tages ist die Geduld,
die Auszeichnung der armselige Stern
der Hoffnung über dem Herzen.

Er wird verliehen,
wenn nichts mehr geschieht,
wenn das Trommelfeuer verstummt,
wenn der Feind unsichtbar geworden ist
und der Schatten ewiger Rüstung
den Himmel bedeckt.

Er wird verliehen
für die Flucht von den Fahnen,
für die Tapferkeit vor dem Freund,
für den Verrat unwürdiger Geheimnisse
und die Nichtachtung
jeglichen Befehls.

Every Day

War is no longer declared,
only continued. The monstrous
has become everyday. The hero
stays away from battle. The weak
have gone to the front.
The uniform of the day is patience,
its medal the pitiful star
of hope above the heart.

The medal is awarded
when nothing more happens,
when the artillery falls silent,
when the enemy has grown invisible
and the shadow of eternal armament
covers the sky.

It is awarded
for desertion of the flag,
for bravery in the face of friends,
for the betrayal of unworthy secrets
and the disregard
of every command.

Botschaft

Aus der leichenwarmen Vorhalle des Himmels tritt die Sonne.
Es sind dort nicht die Unsterblichen,
sondern die Gefallenen, vernehmen wir.

Und Glanz kehrt sich nicht an Verwesung. Unsere Gottheit,
die Geschichte, hat uns ein Grab bestellt,
aus dem es keine Auferstehung gibt.

Message

From the cadaverous warmth of heaven's vestibule
the sun appears.
There are no immortal souls up there,
only the war dead. Or so we hear.

And light pays no heed to decay. Our godhead,
History, has reserved us a grave
from which there is no resurrection.

Die Brücken

Straffer zieht der Wind das Band vor den Brücken.

An den Traversen zerrieb
der Himmel sein dunkelstes Blau.
Hüben und drüben wechseln
im Licht unsre Schatten.

Pont Mirabeau ... Waterloobridge ...
Wie ertragen's die Namen,
die Namenlosen zu tragen?

Von den Verlornen gerührt,
die der Glaube nicht trug,
erwachen die Trommeln im Fluß.

Einsam sind alle Brücken,
und der Ruhm ist ihnen gefährlich
wie uns, vermeinen wir doch,
die Schritte der Sterne
auf unserer Schulter zu spüren.
Doch übers Gefälle des Vergänglichen
wölbt uns kein Traum.

Besser ist's, im Auftrag der Ufer
zu leben, von einem zum andern,
und tagsüber zu wachen,
daß das Band der Berufene trennt.
Denn er erreicht die Schere der Sonne
im Nebel, und wenn sie ihn blendet,
umfängt ihn der Nebel im Fall.

The Bridges

Wind blows the ribbon tighter before the bridges.

The sky grated its deepest blue
along the pilings.
Here and there our shadows
change places in the light.

Pont Mirabeau . . . Waterloo Bridge . . .
How can the names bear
carrying the nameless?

Moved by the lost ones
that faith could not carry,
the drums awaken in the river.

All bridges are lonely.
And fame is just as dangerous for them
as for us, though we think
we feel the tread of stars
on our shoulders.
Yet no dream arches
over the slope of our mortality.

It's better to live for the riverbanks,
crossing from one to the other,
watching all day for the chosen one
to cut the ribbon.
For he reaches the sun shears
wrapped in fog; and should the light blind him,
the fog will cushion his fall.

Nachtflug

Unser Acker ist der Himmel,
im Schweiß der Motoren bestellt,
angesichts der Nacht,
unter Einsatz des Traums –

geträumt auf Schädelstätten und Scheiterhaufen,
unter dem Dach der Welt, dessen Ziegel
der Wind forttrug – und nun Regen, Regen, Regen
in unserem Haus und in den Mühlen
die blinden Flüge der Fledermäuse.
Wer wohnte dort? Wessen Hände waren rein?
Wer leuchtete in der Nacht,
Gespenst den Gespenstern?

Im Stahlgefieder geborgen, verhören
Instrumente den Raum, Kontrolluhren und Skalen
das Wolkengesträuch, und es streift die Liebe
unsres Herzens vergessene Sprache:
kurz und lang lang ... Für eine Stunde
rührt Hagel die Trommel des Ohrs,
das, uns abgeneigt, lauscht und verwindet.

Nicht untergegangen sind Sonne und Erde,
nur als Gestirne gewandert und nicht zu erkennen.

Wir sind aufgestiegen von einem Hafen,
wo Wiederkehr nicht zählt
und nicht Fracht und nicht Fang.
Indiens Gewürze und Seiden aus Japan
gehören den Händlern
wie die Fische den Netzen.

Night Flight

Our field is the sky,
tilled by the sweat of motors,
in the face of night,
at the risk of our dreams—

dreamt at Golgotha and on funeral pyres,
beneath the roof of the world, whose shingles
the wind has carried away—and now rain, rain, rain
in our house, while blind bats
circle in the water mills.
Who lived there? Whose hands were pure?
Who glowed in the night,
a ghost to other ghosts?

Sheltered in steel plumage, instruments
interrogate the air, control clocks and meters
examine cloud thickets, and love grazes
our heart's forgotten language:
short and long long . . . For an hour
hail beats the drum of our ear
which turns away from us, eavesdrops and triumphs.

Sun and earth haven't set—
just wandered off as stars, unrecognizable.

We have risen from a port
where the return home does not count,
nor freight nor catch.
India's spices and silks from Japan
belong to the traders
like fish to the nets.

Doch ein Geruch ist zu spüren,
vorlaufend den Kometen,
und das Gewebe der Luft,
von gefallnen Kometen zerrissen.
Nenn's den Status der Einsamen,
in dem sich das Staunen vollzieht.
Nichts weiter.

Wir sind aufgestiegen, und die Klöster sind leer,
seit wir dulden, ein Orden, der nicht heilt und nicht lehrt.
Zu handeln ist nicht Sache der Piloten. Sie haben
Stützpunkte im Aug und auf den Knien ausgebreitet
die Landkarte einer Welt, der nichts hinzuzufügen ist.

Wer lebt dort unten? Wer weint . . .
Wer verliert den Schlüssel zum Haus?
Wer findet sein Bett nicht, wer schläft
auf den Schwellen? Wer, wenn der Morgen kommt,
wagt's, den Silberstreifen zu deuten: seht, über mir . . .
Wenn das Wasser von neuem ins Mühlrad greift,
wer wagt's, sich der Nacht zu erinnern?

Yet a fragrance can be sensed
ahead of the comets,
and the weave of the air
torn by fallen comets.
Call it the status of the lonely
who still wonder.
Nothing more.

We have risen and the cloisters are empty,
since we have endured, an order that can't save or teach.
Action isn't the pilots' concern. They have their eyes
fixed on defense posts, and spread out on their knees
the map of a world to which nothing can be added.

Who lives down below? Who cries . . .
Who has lost his housekey?
Who can't find his bed, who sleeps
on doorsteps? Who, when morning comes,
will dare to interpret the silver trail: look, above me . . .
When water pushes the mill wheel again,
who will dare to remember the night?

Psalm

1

Schweigt mit mir, wie alle Glocken schweigen!

In der Nachgeburt der Schrecken
sucht das Geschmeiß nach neuer Nahrung.
Zur Ansicht hängt karfreitags eine Hand
am Firmament, zwei Finger fehlen ihr,
sie kann nicht schwören, daß alles,
alles nicht gewesen sei und nichts
sein wird. Sie taucht ins Wolkenrot,
entrückt die neuen Mörder
und geht frei.

Nachts auf dieser Erde
in Fenster greifen, die Linnen zurückschlagen,
daß der Kranken Heimlichkeit bloßliegt,
ein Geschwür voll Nahrung, unendliche Schmerzen
für jeden Geschmack.

Die Metzger halten, behandschuht,
den Atem der Entblößten an,
der Mond in der Tür fällt zu Boden,
laß die Scherben liegen, den Henkel ...

Alles war gerichtet für die letzte Ölung.
(Das Sakrament kann nicht vollzogen werden.)

Psalm

1

Be still with me, as all bells are still!

In the afterbirth of terror
the rabble hunts for new nourishment.
On Good Friday a hand hangs in the sky
on display; it's missing two fingers
and can't swear that everything,
everything didn't happen and nothing
ever will. It dives into red dusk,
carries off the new murderers
and goes free.

At night on this earth
open the windows, fold back the sheets,
lay bare the secrets of the sick,
an ulcer full of nourishment, infinite pain
for every taste.

Butchers put on gloves
and hold the breath of the naked.
The moon in the door falls to the ground,
let the pieces lie, the handle . . .

Everything was prepared for the last anointment.
(The sacrament cannot take place.)

2

Wie eitel alles ist.
Wälze eine Stadt heran,
erhebe dich aus dem Staub dieser Stadt,
übernimm ein Amt
und verstelle dich,
um der Bloßstellung zu entgehen.

Löse die Versprechen ein
vor einem blinden Spiegel in der Luft,
vor einer verschlossenen Tür im Wind.

Unbegangen sind die Wege auf der Steilwand des Himmels.

3

O Augen, an dem Sonnenspeicher Erde verbrannt,
mit der Regenlast aller Augen beladen,
und jetzt versponnen, verwebt
von den tragischen Spinnen
der Gegenwart . . .

4

In die Mulde meiner Stummheit
leg ein Wort
und zieh Wälder groß zu beiden Seiten,
daß mein Mund
ganz im Schatten liegt.

2

How vain everything is.
Roll a city toward you,
rise up from the city's dust,
take office
and mask yourself
to escape exposure.

Honor your promises
before a dull mirror in the air,
before a closed door in the wind.

Untraveled are the paths along the face of the sky.

3

O eyes, burned on the sun silo earth,
heavy with the rain of all eyes,
and now spun, woven
by the tragic spiders
of the present . . .

4

In the hollow of my mute being
place a word—
grow forests thick on either side
so that my mouth
lies all in shade.

Im Gewitter der Rosen

Wohin wir uns wenden im Gewitter der Rosen,
ist die Nacht von Dornen erhellt, und der Donner
des Laubs, das so leise war in den Büschen,
folgt uns jetzt auf dem Fuß.

In the Storm of Roses

Wherever we turn in the storm of roses,
thorns illuminate the night. And the thunder
of a thousand leaves, once so quiet on the bushes,
is right at our heels.

Salz und Brot

Nun schickt der Wind die Schienen voraus,
wir werden folgen in langsamen Zügen
und diese Inseln bewohnen,
Vertrauen gegen Vertrauen.

In die Hand meines ältesten Freunds leg ich
mein Amt zurück; es verwaltet der Regenmann
jetzt mein finsteres Haus und ergänzt
im Schuldbuch die Linien, die ich zog,
seit ich seltener blieb.

Du, im fieberweißen Ornat,
holst die Verbannten ein und reißt
aus dem Fleisch der Kakteen einen Stachel
– das Zeichen der Ohnmacht,
dem wir uns willenlos beugen.

Wir wissen,
daß wir des Kontinentes Gefangene bleiben
und seinen Kränkungen wieder verfallen,
und die Gezeiten der Wahrheit
werden nicht seltener sein.

Schläft doch im Felsen
der wenig erleuchtete Schädel,
die Kralle hängt in der Kralle
im dunklen Gestein, und verheilt
sind die Stigmen am Violett des Vulkans.

Von den großen Gewittern des Lichts
hat keines die Leben erreicht.

Salt and Bread

Now the wind sends the rails ahead.
We shall follow in slow trains
and inhabit these islands,
trust against trust.

I hand back my office to my
oldest friend. Now the rainman administers
my gloomy house, completing the columns
I drew in my debt book
since I stayed less often.

You, in fever-white vestments,
bring in the banished and rip
a thorn out of the cactus flesh
—the sign of helplessness
to which we bow passively.

We know
that we shall stay prisoners of the continent,
victims of its old offenses.
And the tides of truth
will not diminish.

Even though the shadowy skull
sleeps in the rocks,
claw hangs in claw
in the dark stone, and healed
are the stigmata on the violet volcano.

Of the great storms of light
none has reached the living.

So nehm ich vom Salz,
wenn uns das Meer übersteigt,
und kehre zurück
und legs auf die Schwelle
und trete ins Haus.

Wir teilen ein Brot mit dem Regen,
ein Brot, eine Schuld und ein Haus.

So I take the salt
when the sea rises over us,
and turn back,
and place it on the doorsill,
and step inside the house.

We share our bread with the rain—
one bread, one debt and one house.

Große Landschaft bei Wien

Geister der Ebene, Geister des wachsenden Stroms,
zu unsrem Ende gerufen, haltet nicht vor der Stadt!
Nehmt auch mit euch, was vom Wein überhing
auf brüchigen Rändern, und führt an ein Rinnsal,
wen nach Ausweg verlangt, und öffnet die Steppen!

Drüben verkümmert das nackte Gelenk eines Baums,
ein Schwungrad springt ein, aus dem Feld schlagen
die Bohrtürme den Frühling, Statuenwäldern weicht
der verworfene Torso des Grüns, und es wacht
die Iris des Öls über den Brunnen im Land.

Was liegt daran? Wir spielen die Tänze nicht mehr.
Nach langer Pause: Dissonanzen gelichtet, wenig cantabile.
(Und ihren Atem spür ich nicht mehr auf den Wangen!)
Still stehn die Räder. Durch Staub und Wolkenspreu
schleift den Mantel, der unsre Liebe deckte, das Riesenrad.

Nirgends gewährt man, wie hier, vor den ersten Küssen
die letzten. Es gilt, mit dem Nachklang im Mund
weiterzugehn und zu schweigen. Wo der Kranich
im Schilf der flachen Gewässer seinen Bogen vollendet,
tönender als die Welle, schlägt ihm die Stunde im Rohr.

Asiens Atem ist jenseits.

Rhythmischer Aufgang von Saaten, reifer Kulturen
Ernten vorm Untergang, sind sie verbrieft, so weiß ichs
dem Wind noch zu sagen. Hinter der Böschung
trübt weicheres Wasser das Aug, und es will
mich noch anfallen trunkenes Limesgefühl;
unter den Pappeln am Römerstein grab ich

Great Landscape near Vienna

Spirits of the plain, Spirits of the growing river,
summoned for our demise: don't stop before the city!
Take with you whatever wine was left hanging
over crumbling banks; lead toward a stream
whoever demands a way out. And open up the steppes!

Over there the naked crook of a tree withers away,
a fly-wheel starts spinning, the derricks chase
Spring from the field, forests of statues
overpower the abandoned torso of green, and the iris of oil
watches over the woodland wells.

What for? We've stopped playing the dances.
After a long intermission: dissonances clarified, barely
    cantabile.
(And I no longer feel their breath on my cheeks!)
The wheels stand still. Through dust and cloud chaff
the ferris-wheel drags the cloak that covered our love.

Nowhere does one grant, as here, the last kisses
before the first. With a dying song in our mouth
we must travel on and be silent. Among the rushes
of shallow waters the crane completes his arching flight,
ringing more than the waves, and his hour tolls in the reed.

Asia's breath is on the other shore.

Rhythmical sprouting of seedlings, the harvests
of ripe cultures before their fall: though indisputable,
I can still say it to the winds. Behind the slope
softer waters blur my eye, and the drunken feeling
of *Limes* would still assail me.
Among the poplars, beside the Roman stone, I dig

nach dem Schauplatz vielvölkriger Trauer,
nach dem Lächeln Ja und dem Lächeln Nein.

Alles Leben ist abgewandert in Baukästen,
neue Not mildert man sanitär, in den Alleen
blüht die Kastanie duftlos, Kerzenrauch
kostet die Luft nicht wieder, über der Brüstung
im Park weht so einsam das Haar, im Wasser
sinken die Bälle, vorbei an der Kinderhand
bis auf den Grund, und es begegnet
das tote Auge dem blauen, das es einst war.

Wunder des Unglaubens sind ohne Zahl.
Besteht ein Herz darauf, ein Herz zu sein?
Träum, daß du rein bist, heb die Hand zum Schwur,
träum dein Geschlecht, das dich besiegt, träum
und wehr dennoch mystischer Abkehr im Protest.
Mit einer andern Hand gelingen Zahlen
und Analysen, die dich entzaubern.
Was dich trennt, bist du. Verström,
komm wissend wieder, in neuer Abschiedsgestalt.

Dem Orkan voraus fliegt die Sonne nach Westen,
zweitausend Jahre sind um, und uns wird nichts bleiben.
Es hebt der Wind Barockgirlanden auf,
es fällt von den Stiegen das Puttengesicht,
es stürzen Basteien in dämmernde Höfe,
von den Kommoden die Masken und Kränze ...

Nur auf dem Platz im Mittagslicht, mit der Kette
am Säulenfuß und dem vergänglichsten Augenblick
geneigt und der Schönheit verfallen, sag ich mich los
von der Zeit, ein Geist unter Geistern, die kommen.

Maria am Gestade –
das Schiff ist leer, der Stein ist blind,

for the theater of many-peopled sorrow,
for the smile Yes and the smile No.

All life has wandered off into building blocks;
new misfortune is softened sanitarily; in the streets,
chestnut trees bloom ordorlessly, and the air no longer
tastes of candle smoke. Above the ramparts
in the park, locks of hair blow lonely. Balls sink
in the water past children's hands
down to the bottom; and the dead eye meets
the blue one it used to be.

The miracles of unbelief are infinite.
Does a heart insist on being a heart?
Dream that you are pure, lift your hand to swear,
dream of the lineage which conquers you, dream of
and yet—protesting—resist the mystical retreat.
Your other hand succeeds with numbers
and analyses that break your enchantment.
You are what divides you. Stream on,
come back wise, in a new form for departing.

The sun flies ahead of the hurricane to the west.
Two thousand years are up and nothing will be left to us.
The wind lifts up baroque garlands,
a cherub's face falls from the stairs,
bastions cave in on evening courtyards,
masks and wreathes drop from the dressers . . .

Only in the square's noon light, with a chain
around the column foot, and bowed to the most fleeting
moment, a captive of beauty: I set myself free
from time, a spirit among spirits who are coming.

Our Lady on the Shore—
the nave is empty, the stone is blind,

gerettet ist keiner, getroffen sind viele,
das Öl will nicht brennen, wir haben
alle davon getrunken – wo bleibt
dein ewiges Licht?

So sind auch die Fische tot und treiben
den schwarzen Meeren zu, die uns erwarten.
Wir aber mündeten längst, vom Sog
anderer Ströme ergriffen, wo die Welt
ausblieb und wenig Heiterkeit war.
Die Türme der Ebene rühmen uns nach,
daß wir willenlos kamen und auf den Stufen
der Schwermut fielen und tiefer fielen,
mit dem scharfen Gehör für den Fall.

no one is saved, many are wounded,
the oil will not burn, we have all
drunk from it—where is
your eternal light?

The fish are also dead and drift
into the black seas awaiting us.
But we have long since reached the sea, gripped
by the tow of other currents, where the world
was missing and few were merry.
The towers of the plain praise us,
for we came passively, falling on the steps
of melancholy, falling deeper,
with an ear sharp for the fall.

FROM THE COLLECTION
Invocation of the Great Bear

Das Spiel ist aus

Mein lieber Bruder, wann bauen wir uns ein Floß
und fahren den Himmel hinunter?
Mein lieber Bruder, bald ist die Fracht zu groß
und wir gehen unter.

Mein lieber Bruder, wir zeichnen aufs Papier
viele Länder und Schienen.
Gib acht, vor den schwarzen Linien hier
fliegst du hoch mit den Minen.

Mein lieber Bruder, dann will ich an den Pfahl
gebunden sein und schreien.
Doch du reitest schon aus dem Totental
und wir fliehen zu zweien.

Wach im Zigeunerlager und wach im Wüstenzelt,
es rinnt uns der Sand aus den Haaren,
dein und mein Alter und das Alter der Welt
mißt man nicht mit den Jahren.

Laß dich von listigen Raben, von klebriger Spinnenhand
und der Feder im Strauch nicht betrügen,
iß und trink auch nicht im Schlaraffenland,
es schäumt Schein in den Pfannen und Krügen.

Nur wer an der goldenen Brücke für die Karfunkelfee
das Wort noch weiß, hat gewonnen.
Ich muß dir sagen, es ist mit dem letzten Schnee
im Garten zerronnen.

Von vielen, vielen Steinen sind unsre Füße so wund.
Einer heilt. Mit dem wollen wir springen,

The Game Is Over

My dearest brother, when will we build a raft
and sail down the sky?
My dearest brother, soon the freight will be too big
and we will sink and die.

My dearest brother, we'll draw maps
of many lands and railway lines.
Watch out, here in front of the tracks
you'll be blown up with the mines.

My dearest brother, then I want to be tied
to a stake and scream with all my might.
But out of the valley of death you ride
and together we take flight.

Awake in the gypsy camp and the desert tent,
sand runs out of our hair like tears.
Your age and my age and the age of the earth
cannot be measured in years.

Don't be fooled by the ravens, the sticky hand
of the spider or the feather in the shrubs.
Don't eat or drink in Never-Never-Land,
falsehood foams in skillets and jugs.

On the golden bridge only the one who knows
the fairy's word can win.
I must tell you, with the last snows
it melted in the garden.

From many, many stones our feet are sore.
One will heal. Let's jump with it till the fairytale king,

bis der Kinderkönig, mit dem Schlüssel zu seinem Reich
   im Mund,
uns holt, und wir werden singen:

Es ist eine schöne Zeit, wenn der Dattelkern keimt!
Jeder, der fällt, hat Flügel.
Roter Fingerhut ist's, der den Armen das Leichentuch
   säumt,
und dein Herzblatt sinkt auf mein Siegel.

Wir müssen schlafen gehn, Liebster, das Spiel ist aus.
Auf Zehenspitzen. Die weißen Hemden bauschen.
Vater und Mutter sagen, es geistert im Haus,
wenn wir den Atem tauschen.

holding in his mouth the key to the castle door,
takes us away and we sing:

It's a happy time when the date pit blooms,
everyone who falls has wings.
Red Thimble hems the shrouds in the poor men's tombs,
onto my seal your young leaf sinks.

The game is over, dearest, it's time for prayers.
We go on tiptoe, our nightshirts billowing and white.
Father and Mother say there're ghosts upstairs,
when we trade our breaths at night.

Anrufung des Großen Bären

Großer Bär, komm herab, zottige Nacht,
Wolkenpelztier mit den alten Augen,
Sternenaugen,
durch das Dickicht brechen schimmernd
deine Pfoten mit den Krallen,
Sternenkrallen,
wachsam halten wir die Herden,
doch gebannt von dir, und mißtrauen
deinen müden Flanken und den scharfen
halbentblößten Zähnen,
alter Bär.

Ein Zapfen: eure Welt.
Ihr: die Schuppen dran.
Ich treib sie, roll sie
von den Tannen im Anfang
zu den Tannen am Ende,
schnaub sie an, prüf sie im Maul
und pack zu mit den Tatzen.

Fürchtet euch oder fürchtet euch nicht!
Zahlt in den Klingelbeutel und gebt
dem blinden Mann ein gutes Wort,
daß er den Bären an der Leine hält.
Und würzt die Lämmer gut.

's könnt sein, daß dieser Bär
sich losreißt, nicht mehr droht
und alle Zapfen jagt, die von den Tannen
gefallen sind, den großen, geflügelten,
die aus dem Paradiese stürzten.

Invocation of the Great Bear

Great Bear, come down, shaggy night,
cloud-coated beast with the old eyes,
star eyes.
Through the thickets your paws break
shimmering with their claws,
star claws.
We guard our herds with a watchful eye,
though caught in your spell, and mistrust
your tired flanks and sharp,
half-bared fangs,
old bear.

A pine cone: your world.
You: its scales.
I hunt them, roll them
from the pines in the beginning
to the pines at the end.
Snort on them, test them with my muzzle
and set to work with my paws.

Be afraid or don't be afraid!
Just drop your coins in the collection basket and give
the blind man a good word,
let him hold the bear on its leash.
And spice the lambs well.

Perhaps this bear
will break loose, stop threatening
and chase all the cones that have fallen
from the pines, from the great, winged ones
hurled down from Paradise.

Mein Vogel

Was auch geschieht: die verheerte Welt
sinkt in die Dämmrung zurück,
einen Schlaftrunk halten ihr die Wälder bereit,
und vom Turm, den der Wächter verließ,
blicken ruhig und stet die Augen der Eule herab.

Was auch geschieht: du weißt deine Zeit,
mein Vogel, nimmst deinen Schleier
und fliegst durch den Nebel zu mir.

Wir äugen im Dunstkreis, den das Gelichter bewohnt.
Du folgst meinem Wink, stößt hinaus
und wirbelst Gefieder und Fell –

Mein eisgrauer Schultergenoß, meine Waffe,
mit jener Feder besteckt, meiner einzigen Waffe!
Mein einziger Schmuck: Schleier und Feder von dir.

Wenn auch im Nadeltanz unterm Baum
die Haut mir brennt
und der hüfthohe Strauch
mich mit würzigen Blättern versucht,
wenn meine Locke züngelt,
sich wiegt und nach Feuchte verzehrt,
stürzt mir der Sterne Schutt
doch genau auf das Haar.

Wenn ich vom Rauch behelmt
wieder weiß, was geschieht,
mein Vogel, mein Beistand des Nachts,
wenn ich befeuert bin in der Nacht,
knistert's im dunklen Bestand,
und ich schlage den Funken aus mir.

My Bird

Whatever comes to pass: the devastated world
sinks back into twilight,
the forest offers it a sleeping potion,
and from the tower the watchman's forsaken,
peaceful and constant the eyes of the owl stare down.

Whatever comes to pass: you know your time,
my bird, you put on your veil
and fly through the mist to me.

We peer into the haze where the rabble houses.
You follow my nod and storm out
in a whirl of feathers and fur—

My ice-gray shoulder companion, my weapon,
adorned with a feather, my only weapon!
My only finery: your veil and your feather.

And even when my skin burns
in the needle dance beneath the tree,
and the hip-high shrubs
tempt me with their spicy leaves,
when my curls dart like snake tongues,
sway and long for moisture,
the dust of distant stars still falls
right on my hair.

When I, in a helmet of smoke,
come back to my senses,
my bird, my nighttime ally,
when I'm ablaze in the night,
the dark grove crackles
and I hammer the spark from my limbs.

Wenn ich befeuert bleib wie ich bin
und vom Feuer geliebt,
bis das Harz aus den Stämmen tritt,
auf die Wunden träufelt und warm
die Erde verspinnt,
(und wenn du mein Herz auch ausraubst des Nachts,
mein Vogel auf Glauben und mein Vogel auf Treu!)
rückt jene Warte ins Licht,
die du, besänftigt,
in herrlicher Ruhe erfliegst –
was auch geschieht.

And when I stay ablaze as I am,
loved by the flame
until the resin streams out of the trunks,
drips over the wounds and
spins the earth warm into thread
(and though you rob my heart at night,
my bird of belief, my bird of faith!),
the watchtower moves into brightness
where you, tranquil now,
alight in magnificent peace—
whatever comes to pass.

Landnahme

Ins Weideland kam ich,
als es schon Nacht war,
in den Wiesen die Narben witternd
und den Wind, eh er sich regte.
Die Liebe graste nicht mehr,
die Glocken waren verhallt
und die Büschel verhärmt.

Ein Horn stak im Land,
vom Leittier verrannt,
ins Dunkel gerammt.

Aus der Erde zog ich's,
zum Himmel hob ich's
mit ganzer Kraft.

Um dieses Land mit Klängen
ganz zu erfüllen,
stieß ich ins Horn,
willens im kommenden Wind
und unter den wehenden Halmen
jeder Herkunft zu leben!

A New Land

I came into pasture land
when night had fallen,
sniffing out the scars in the meadows,
scenting the wind before it rose.
Love grazed no longer,
the bells had stopped ringing
and the sheaves were dry and worn.

A horn was stuck into the earth,
rammed there by the herd's leader,
hammered into the dark.

I drew it from the earth,
I lifted it to the sky
with all my strength.

To fill this land
with music
I blew the horn,
ready to live in the coming wind
among the waving grasses
of every origin!

Curriculum Vitae

Lang ist die Nacht,
lang für den Mann,
der nicht sterben kann, lang
unter Straßenlaternen schwankt
sein nacktes Aug und sein Aug
schnapsatemblind, und Geruch
von nassem Fleisch unter seinen Nägeln
betäubt ihn nicht immer, o Gott,
lang ist die Nacht.

Mein Haar wird nicht weiß,
denn ich kroch aus dem Schoß von Maschinen,
Rosenrot strich mir Teer auf die Stirn
und die Strähnen, man hatt' ihr
die schneeweiße Schwester erwürgt. Aber ich,
der Häuptling, schritt durch die Stadt
von zehnmalhunderttausend Seelen, und mein Fuß
trat auf die Seelenasseln unterm Lederhimmel,
    aus dem
zehnmalhunderttausend Friedenspfeifen
hingen, kalt. Engelsruhe
wünscht' ich mir oft
und Jagdgründe, voll
vom ohnmächtigen Geschrei
meiner Freunde.

Mit gespreizten Beinen und Flügeln,
binsenweis stieg die Jugend
über mich, über Jauche, über Jasmin ging's
in die riesigen Nächte mit dem Quadrat-
wurzelgeheimnis, es haucht die Sage
des Tods stündlich mein Fenster an,
Wolfsmilch gebt mir und schüttet

Curriculum Vitae

Long is the night,
long for the man
who cannot die, long
has his naked eye tottered
under street lamps, his eye
blinded with whiskey breath, and the smell
of wet flesh under his nails
doesn't always kill the pain, oh God,
long is the night.

My hair won't turn white
for I crawled from a womb of machines,
Rose Red smeared tar on my forehead
and curls, someone had strangled
her snow-white sister. But I,
the chief, strode through the city
of ten times a hundred thousand spirits, and my feet
trod on spirit lice beneath a leather sky, from which
ten times a hundred thousand peace pipes
were hanging, cold. The repose of angels
is what I've often wished for,
and hunting grounds filled
with the helpless wailing
of my friends.

With spread-eagled legs and wings,
the young ones overwhelm me with
platitudes, over dung and daisies they went
into those giant nights with their square-root
secret, the legend of death
fogs my window hourly with its breath.
Give me spurge milk and pour
the laughter of the old

in meinen Rachen das Lachen
der Alten vor mir, wenn ich in Schlaf
fall über den Folianten,
in den beschämenden Traum,
daß ich nicht taug für Gedanken,
mit Troddeln spiel,
aus denen Schlangen fransen.

Auch unsere Mütter haben
von der Zukunft ihrer Männer geträumt,
sie haben sie mächtig gesehen,
revolutionär und einsam,
doch nach der Andacht im Garten
über das flammende Unkraut gebeugt,
Hand in Hand mit dem geschwätzigen
Kind ihrer Liebe. Mein trauriger Vater,
warum habt ihr damals geschwiegen
und nicht weitergedacht?

Verloren in den Feuerfontänen,
in einer Nacht neben einem Geschütz,
das nicht feuert, verdammt lang
ist die Nacht, unter dem Auswurf
des gelbsüchtigen Monds, seinem galligen
Licht, fegt in der Machttraumspur
über mich (das halt ich nicht ab)
der Schlitten mit der verbrämten
Geschichte hinweg.
Nicht daß ich schlief: wach war ich,
zwischen Eisskeletten sucht' ich den Weg,
kam heim, wand mir Efeu
um Arm und Bein und weißte
mit Sonnenresten die Ruinen.
Ich hielt die hohen Feiertage,
und erst wenn es gelobt war,
brach ich das Brot.

in my muzzle, when sleeping
I trip over folios
in the shameful dream
that I'm not fit for thoughts,
that I'm playing with tassels
whose fringes are vipers.

Even our mothers have
dreamed of their men's futures,
imagined them as mighty
revolutionaries, lonely,
yet bent over the flaming bush
after prayers in the garden,
hand in hand with the babbling
child of their love. My sad father,
why were you so silent then,
nor ever thought past tomorrow?

Lost in the flaming fountains,
in a night beside a cannon
that won't fire, damned long
is the night, beneath the refuse
of the jaundiced moon, its bilious
light, the sled with its embellished
history rushes over me (I can't stop it)
in the trail of power dreams.
Not that I was sleeping: I was awake,
seeking the way between ice skeletons,
I came home, wound ivy
about my arms and legs, and painted
the ruins white with leftover sun.
I observed the holy days,
and only when it had been blessed
did I break the bread.

In einer großspurigen Zeit
muß man rasch von einem Licht
ins andre gehen, von einem Land
ins andre, unterm Regenbogen,
die Zirkelspitze im Herzen,
zum Radius genommen die Nacht.
Weit offen. Von den Bergen
sieht man Seen, in den Seen
Berge, und im Wolkengestühl
schaukeln die Glocken
der einen Welt. Wessen Welt
zu wissen, ist mir verboten.

An einem Freitag geschah's
– ich fastete um mein Leben,
die Luft troff vom Saft der Zitronen
und die Gräte stak mir im Gaumen –
da löst' ich aus dem entfalteten Fisch
einen Ring, der, ausgeworfen
bei meiner Geburt, in den Strom
der Nacht fiel und versank.
Ich warf ihn zurück in die Nacht.

O hätt ich nicht Todesfurcht!
Hätt ich das Wort,
(verfehlt ich's nicht),
hätt ich nicht Disteln im Herz,
(schlüg ich die Sonne aus),
hätt ich nicht Gier im Mund,
(tränk ich das wilde Wasser nicht),
schlüg ich die Wimper nicht auf,
(hätt ich die Schnur nicht gesehn).

In an arrogant age
we must rush from one light
to the next, from one land
into the next, beneath the rainbow,
the compass points in our heart
and the night as radius.
Wide open. From the mountains
lakes can be seen, in the oceans
mountains, and in the cloud-pews
bells of the one world
are swaying. Whose world
I am forbidden to know.

It happened on a Friday
—I was fasting for my life,
the air oozed with the juice of lemons
and a fish bone stuck in my gums—
from the gutted fish
I took out a ring, which,
discarded at my birth, fell
into the river of night and sank.
I threw it back into the night.

If only I had no fear of death!
If I had the word
(I wouldn't miss it),
if I hadn't thistles in my heart
(I wouldn't beat out the sun),
if I hadn't greed in my mouth
(I wouldn't drink the wild water)
if I didn't open my eyelids
(I wouldn't have seen the rope).

Ziehn sie den Himmel fort?
Trüg mich die Erde nicht,
läg ich schon lange still,
läg ich schon lang,
wo die Nacht mich will,
eh sie die Nüstern bläht
und ihren Huf hebt
zu neuen Schlägen,
immer zum Schlag.
Immer die Nacht.
Und kein Tag.

Are they dragging away the sky?
If the Earth hadn't carried me
I'd long be lying still,
I'd long be lying
where the night wants me,
before she flares her nostrils
and lifts her hoof
to smite me,
always to smite.
Always the night.
And no day.

Nebelland

Im Winter ist meine Geliebte
unter den Tieren des Waldes.
Daß ich vor Morgen zurückmuß,
weiß die Füchsin und lacht.
Wie die Wolken erzittern! Und mir
auf den Schneekragen fällt
eine Lage von brüchigem Eis.

Im Winter ist meine Geliebte
ein Baum unter Bäumen und lädt
die glückverlassenen Krähen
ein in ihr schönes Geäst. Sie weiß,
daß der Wind, wenn es dämmert,
ihr starres, mit Reif besetztes
Abendkleid hebt und mich heimjagt.

Im Winter ist meine Geliebte
unter den Fischen und stumm.
Hörig den Wassern, die der Strich
ihrer Flossen von innen bewegt,
steh ich am Ufer und seh,
bis mich Schollen vertreiben,
wie sie taucht und sich wendet.

Und wieder vom Jagdruf des Vogels
getroffen, der seine Schwingen
über mir steift, stürz ich
auf offenem Feld: sie entfiedert
die Hühner und wirft mir ein weißes
Schlüsselbein zu. Ich nehm's um den Hals
und geh fort durch den bitteren Flaum.

Land of Fog

In winter my love
is among the beasts of the forest.
The vixen knows
I must be back before morning
and she laughs.
How the clouds tremble! And a layer
of brittle ice falls
on my snow collar.

In winter my love
is a tree among trees
and invites the hapless crows
to nest in her beautiful boughs. She knows
that the wind, when evening falls,
will lift her stiff, frost-embroidered
evening dress and chase me home.

In winter my love
is among the fish and cannot speak.
A slave to the waters her fins
stroke from within,
I stand on the bank and watch,
till ice floes drive me away,
how she dives and turns.

And struck once more by the hunting cry
of the bird stiffening
his wings above me, I fall
on an open field: she plucks
the hens and tosses me a white
collar bone. I place it around my neck
and go forth through the bitter down.

Treulos ist meine Geliebte,
ich weiß, sie schwebt manchmal
auf hohen Schuh'n nach der Stadt,
sie küßt in den Bars mit dem Strohhalm
die Gläser tief auf den Mund,
und es kommen ihr Worte für alle.
Doch diese Sprache verstehe ich nicht.

Nebelland hab ich gesehen,
Nebelherz hab ich gegessen.

Faithless is my love,
I know, sometimes she sways
on high heels into town,
kissing bar glasses with her straw
deep in their mouths,
finding the right words for everyone.
But I don't understand this language.

It is fog land I have seen,
fog heart I have eaten.

Erklär mir, Liebe

Dein Hut lüftet sich leis, grüßt, schwebt im Wind,
dein unbedeckter Kopf hat's Wolken angetan,
dein Herz hat anderswo zu tun,
dein Mund verleibt sich neue Sprachen ein,
das Zittergras im Land nimmt überhand,
Sternblumen bläst der Sommer an und aus,
von Flocken blind erhebst du dein Gesicht,
du lachst und weinst und gehst an dir zugrund,
was soll dir noch geschehen –

Erklär mir, Liebe!

Der Pfau, in feierlichem Staunen, schlägt sein Rad,
die Taube stellt den Federkragen hoch,
vom Gurren überfüllt, dehnt sich die Luft,
der Entrich schreit, vom wilden Honig nimmt
das ganze Land, auch im gesetzten Park
hat jedes Beet ein goldner Staub umsäumt.

Der Fisch errötet, überholt den Schwarm
und stürzt durch Grotten ins Korallenbett.
Zur Silbersandmusik tanzt scheu der Skorpion.
Der Käfer riecht die Herrlichste von weit;
hätt ich nur seinen Sinn, ich fühlte auch,
daß Flügel unter ihrem Panzer schimmern,
und nähm den Weg zum fernen Erdbeerstrauch!

Erklär mir, Liebe!

Wasser weiß zu reden,
die Welle nimmt die Welle an der Hand,
im Weinberg schwillt die Traube, springt und fällt.
So arglos tritt die Schnecke aus dem Haus!

Tell Me, Love

Your hat lifts up lightly, says hello, sways in the wind,
your uncovered head has touched the clouds,
your heart has business elsewhere,
your mouth imbibes new languages,
the quaking grass is gaining ground,
summer blows star flowers on and off,
blinded by flakes you raise your face,
you laugh and cry and die by your own hand,
what more can yet befall you—

Tell me, love!

The peacock, in ceremonious amazement, spreads its tail,
the dove pulls up its feather collar,
filled with cooing the air expands,
the duck cries, the whole land eats
wild honey, even in the calm park
every flower bed is bordered with gold dust.

The fish blushes, overtakes the school
and tumbles through grottos into a coral bed.
The scorpion dances shyly to silver sand music.
The beetle smells his lover from afar;
if only I had their sense, I'd also feel
how wings shimmer under their shells
and I'd take the path to distant strawberry patches!

Tell me, love!

Water talks,
the wave takes a wave by the hand,
the grape swells in the vineyard, jumps and falls.
The snail steps so unsuspecting from its house.

Ein Stein weiß einen andern zu erweichen!

Erklär mir, Liebe, was ich nicht erklären kann:
sollt ich die kurze schauerliche Zeit
nur mit Gedanken Umgang haben und allein
nichts Liebes kennen und nichts Liebes tun?
Muß einer denken? Wird er nicht vermißt?

Du sagst: es zählt ein andrer Geist auf ihn...
Erklär mir nichts. Ich seh den Salamander
durch jedes Feuer gehen.
Kein Schauer jagt ihn, und es schmerzt ihn nichts.

A stone knows how to soften a stone!

Tell me, love, what I can't explain:
Should I spend this short, horrid time
with thoughts only, and alone
know no love and give none?
Must one think? Won't he be missed?

You say: another spirit is counting on him . . .
Tell me nothing. I see the salamander
pass through every fire.
No horror hounds him, and he feels no pain.

Reklame

Wohin aber gehen wir
ohne sorge sei ohne sorge
wenn es dunkel und wenn es kalt wird
sei ohne sorge
aber
mit musik
was sollen wir tun
heiter und mit musik
und denken
heiter
angesichts eines Endes
mit musik
und wohin tragen wir
am besten
unsre Fragen und den Schauer aller Jahre
in die Traumwäscherei ohne sorge sei ohne sorge
was aber geschieht
am besten
wenn Totenstille

eintritt

Advertisement

But where are we going
you haven't a care not a care
when it grows dark and when it grows cold
you haven't a care
but
with music
what should we do
merrily and with music
and think
merrily
with regard to an end
with music
and where should we carry
best of all
our questions and the shudder of all these years
in the dream laundry you haven't a care not a care
but what happens
best of all
when dead silence

sets in

Rede und Nachrede

Komm nicht aus unsrem Mund,
Wort, das den Drachen sät.
's ist wahr, die Luft ist schwül,
vergoren und gesäuert schäumt das Licht,
und überm Sumpf hängt schwarz der Mückenflor.

Der Schierling bechert gern.
Ein Katzenfell liegt aus,
die Schlange faucht darauf,
der Skorpion tanzt an.

Dring nicht an unser Ohr,
Gerücht von andrer Schuld,
Wort, stirb im Sumpf,
aus dem der Tümpel quillt.

Wort, sei bei uns
von zärtlicher Geduld
und Ungeduld. Es muß dies Säen
ein Ende nehmen!

Dem Tier beikommen wird nicht, wer den Tierlaut
 nachahmt.
Wer seines Betts Geheimnis preisgibt, verwirkt sich alle
 Liebe.
Des Wortes Bastard dient dem Witz, um einen Törichten
 zu opfern.

Wer wünscht von dir ein Urteil über diesen Fremden?
Und fällst du's unverlangt, geh du von Nacht zu Nacht
mit seinen Schwären an den Füßen weiter, geh! komm
 nicht wieder.

Word and Afterword

Come not from our mouth,
word that sows the dragon.
It's true, the air is heavy,
light foams vinegary and stale,
and above the swamp hangs a swarm of black mosquitos.

The hemlock loves to tipple.
A cat skin lies on display.
The snake hisses at it,
the scorpion put in an appearance.

Come not to our ears,
rumor of another sin,
word, die in the swamp
where a muddy pool begins.

Word, stay by us
with tender patience
and impatience. This sowing
must come to an end!

Whoever simulates an animal cry, won't get at the animal.
Whoever betrays the secret of his bed, forfeits all love.
The word's bastard serves the joke to sacrifice a fool.

Who asks you to judge this foreigner?
And should you judge him unasked, go then from night to night
with his sores on your feet, go! Never come back.

Wort, sei von uns,
freisinnig, deutlich, schön.
Gewiß muß es ein Ende nehmen,
sich vorzusehen.

(Der Krebs zieht sich zurück,
der Maulwurf schläft zu lang,
das weiche Wasser löst
den Kalk, der Steine spann.)

Komm, Gunst aus Laut und Hauch,
befestig diesen Mund,
wenn seine Schwachheit uns
entsetzt und hemmt.

Komm und versag dich nicht,
da wir im Streit mit soviel Übel stehen.
Eh Drachenblut den Widersacher schützt,
fällt diese Hand ins Feuer.
Mein Wort, errette mich!

Word, be one of us,
enlightened, distinct, beautiful.
Certainly an end must come
to its cautious living.

(The crab pulls back,
the mole oversleeps,
soft water unties the stones
that lime once wove.)

Come, favor of sound and breath,
make fast this mouth
when its weakness frightens
and chokes us.

Come and do not fail,
for we stand in strife with so much evil.
Ere dragon blood protects our adversary,
this hand will fall into the fire.
You, my word, deliver me!

Das erstgeborene Land

In mein erstgeborenes Land, in den Süden
zog ich und fand, nackt und verarmt
und bis zum Gürtel im Meer,
Stadt und Kastell.

Vom Staub in den Schlaf getreten
lag ich im Licht,
und vom ionischen Salz belaubt
hing ein Baumskelett über mir.

Da fiel kein Traum herab.

Da blüht kein Rosmarin,
kein Vogel frischt
sein Lied in Quellen auf.

In meinem erstgeborenen Land, im Süden
sprang die Viper mich an
und das Grausen im Licht.

O schließ
die Augen schließ!
Preß den Mund auf den Biß!

Und als ich mich selber trank
und mein erstgeborenes Land
die Erdbeben wiegten,
war ich zum Schauen erwacht.

Da fiel mir Leben zu.

Da ist der Stein nicht tot.
Der Docht schnellt auf,
wenn ihn ein Blick entzündet.

The Firstborn Land

To my firstborn land, to the South
I went—and found, naked and poor,
and up to their waist in the sea,
city and castle.

Trodden by dust into sleep,
I lay in light.
Covered with Ionian salt,
the skeleton of a tree hung over me.

No dream fell down.

No rosemary blooms there,
no bird refreshes
its song in the fountain.

In my firstborn land, in the South
the viper pounced at me
with a shudder in the light.

Oh close
your eyes, close them!
Press your mouth against the bite.

And as I drank myself,
and the earthquakes rocked
my firstborn land,
my eyes awoke.

Life fell down to me.

There the stone isn't dead.
The wick flies up
when a glance sets it alight.

Lieder von einer Insel

Schattenfrüchte fallen von den Wänden,
Mondlicht tüncht das Haus, und Asche
erkalteter Krater trägt der Meerwind herein.

In den Umarmungen schöner Knaben
schlafen die Küsten,
dein Fleisch besinnt sich auf meins,
es war mir schon zugetan,
als sich die Schiffe
vom Land lösten und Kreuze
mit unsrer sterblichen Last
Mastendienst taten.

Nun sind die Richtstätten leer,
sie suchen und finden uns nicht.

———

Wenn du auferstehst,
wenn ich aufersteh,
ist kein Stein vor dem Tor,
liegt kein Boot auf dem Meer.

Morgen rollen die Fässer
sonntäglichen Wellen entgegen,
wir kommen auf gesalbten
Sohlen zum Strand, waschen
die Trauben und stampfen
die Ernte zu Wein,
morgen am Strand.

Wenn du auferstehst,
wenn ich aufersteh,
hängt der Henker am Tor,
sinkt der Hammer ins Meer.

———

Songs from an Island

Shadow fruit is falling from the walls,
moonlight bathes the house in white, and the ash
of extinct craters is born in by the sea wind.

In the embrace of handsome youths
the coasts are sleeping.
Your flesh remembers mine,
it was already inclined to me,
when the ships
loosened themselves from shore and the cross
of our mortal burden
kept watch in the rigging.

Now the execution sites are empty,
they search but cannot find us.

———

When you rise from the dead,
when I rise from the dead,
no stone will lie before the gate,
no boat will rest on the sea.

Tomorrow the casks will roll
toward Sunday waves,
we come on anointed
soles to the shore, wash
the grapes and stamp
the harvest into wine,
tomorrow, on the shore.

When you rise from the dead,
when I rise from the dead,
the hangman will hang at the gate,
the hammer will sink into the sea.

———

Einmal muß das Fest ja kommen!
Heiliger Antonius, der du gelitten hast,
heiliger Leonhard, der du gelitten hast,
heiliger Vitus, der du gelitten hast.

Platz unsren Bitten, Platz den Betern,
Platz der Musik und der Freude!
Wir haben Einfalt gelernt,
wir singen im Chor der Zikaden,
wir essen und trinken,
die mageren Katzen
streichen um unseren Tisch,
bis die Abendmesse beginnt,
halt ich dich an der Hand
mit den Augen,
und ein ruhiges mutiges Herz
opfert dir seine Wünsche.

Honig und Nüsse den Kindern,
volle Netze den Fischern,
Fruchtbarkeit den Gärten,
Mond dem Vulkan, Mond dem Vulkan!

Unsre Funken setzten über die Grenzen,
über die Nacht schlugen Raketen
ein Rad, auf dunklen Flößen
entfernt sich die Prozession und räumt
der Vorwelt die Zeit ein,
den schleichenden Echsen,
der schlemmenden Pflanze,
dem fiebernden Fisch,
den Orgien des Winds und der Lust
des Bergs, wo ein frommer
Stern sich verirrt, ihm auf die Brust
schlägt und zerstäubt.

One day the feast must come!
Saint Anthony, you who have suffered,
Saint Leonard, you who have suffered,
Saint Vitus, you who have suffered.

Make way for our prayers, way for the worshippers,
room for music and joy!
We have learned simplicity,
we sing in the choir of cicadas,
we eat and drink,
the lean cats
rub against our table,
until evening mass begins
I hold your hand
with my eyes,
and a quiet, brave heart
sacrifices its wishes to you.

Honey and nuts for the children,
teeming nets for the fishermen,
fertility for the gardens,
moon for the volcano, moon for the volcano!

Our sparks leapt over the borders,
above the night fireworks fanned their
tails, the procession
floats away on dark rafts and gives
time to the primeval world,
to the plodding lizards,
to the carniverous plant,
to the feverish fish,
to the orgies of wind and the lust
of mountains where a pious
star loses its way, collides with their face
and dissolves into dust.

Jetzt seid standhaft, törichte Heilige,
sagt dem Festland, daß die Krater nicht ruhn!
Heiliger Rochus, der du gelitten hast,
o der du gelitten hast, heiliger Franz.

———

Wenn einer fortgeht, muß er den Hut
mit den Muscheln, die er sommerüber
gesammelt hat, ins Meer werfen
und fahren mit wehendem Haar,
er muß den Tisch, den er seiner Liebe
deckte, ins Meer stürzen,
er muß den Rest des Weins,
der im Glas blieb, ins Meer schütten,
er muß den Fischen sein Brot geben
und einen Tropfen Blut ins Meer mischen,
er muß sein Messer gut in die Wellen treiben
und seinen Schuh versenken,
Herz, Anker und Kreuz,
und fahren mit wehendem Haar!
Dann wird er wiederkommen.
Wann?
    Frag nicht.

———

Es ist Feuer unter der Erde,
und das Feuer ist rein.

Es ist Feuer unter der Erde
und flüssiger Stein.

Es ist ein Strom unter der Erde,
der strömt in uns ein.

Stand firm, you foolish saints.
Tell the mainland the craters aren't resting!
Saint Roch, you who have suffered,
oh you who have suffered, Saint Francis.

———

When someone departs he must throw his hat,
filled with the mussels he spent the summer
gathering, in the sea
and sail off with his hair in the wind,
he must hurl the table,
set for his love, in the sea,
he must pour the wine,
left in his glass, into the sea,
he must give his bread to the fish
and mix a drop of his blood with the sea,
he must drive his knife deep into the waves
and sink his shoes,
heart, anchor and cross,
and sail off with his hair in the wind.
Then he will return.
When?
      Do not ask.

———

There is fire under the earth,
and the fire is pure.

There is fire under the earth
and molten rock.

There is a torrent under the earth,
it will stream into us.

Es ist ein Strom unter der Erde,
der sengt das Gebein.

Es kommt ein großes Feuer,
es kommt ein Strom über die Erde.

Wir werden Zeugen sein.

There is a torrent under the earth,
it will scorch our bones.

A great fire is coming,
a torrent is coming over the earth.

We shall be witnesses.

Römisches Nachtbild

Wenn das Schaukelbrett die sieben Hügel
nach oben entführt, gleitet es auch,
von uns beschwert und umschlungen,
ins finstere Wasser,

taucht in den Flußschlamm, bis in unsrem Schoß
die Fische sich sammeln.
Ist die Reihe an uns,
stoßen wir ab.

Es sinken die Hügel,
wir steigen und teilen
jeden Fisch mit der Nacht.

Keiner springt ab.
So gewiß ist's, daß nur die Liebe
und einer den andern erhöht.

Night Portrait of Rome

When the swing abducts the seven hills
into the sky, it will fall back,
heavy with our embraces,
into dark water,

dive in the river mire until fish
gather in our lap.
When it's our turn
we push off.

The hills are sinking;
we climb and share
each fish with the night.

No one jumps off.
For we know: only love
and the hand of a friend
can lift us high.

In Apulien

Unter den Olivenbäumen schüttet Licht die Samen aus,
Mohn erscheint und flackert wieder,
fängt das Öl und brennt es nieder,
und das Licht geht nie mehr aus.

Trommeln in den Höhlenstädten trommeln ohne Unterlaß,
weißes Brot und schwarze Lippen,
Kinder in den Futterkrippen
will der Fliegenschwarm zum Fraß.

Käm die Helle von den Feldern in den Troglodytentag,
könnt der Mohn aus Lampen rauchen,
Schmerz im Schlaf ihn ganz verbrauchen,
bis er nicht mehr brennen mag.

Esel stünden auf und trügen Wasserschläuche übers Land,
Schnüre stickten alle Hände,
Glas und Perlen für die Wände –
Tür im klingenden Gewand.

Die Madonnen stillten Kinder und der Büffel ging' vorbei,
Rauch im Horn, zur grünen Tränke,
endlich reichten die Geschenke:
Lammblut, Fisch und Schlangenei.

Endlich malmen Steine Früchte, und die Krüge sind
    gebrannt.
Öl rinnt offnen Augs herunter,
und der Mohn geht trunken unter,
von Taranteln überrannt.

In Apulia

Light pours out its seed beneath the olive trees,
poppies shoot up and start to flicker,
take the oil they need to burn,
and their light will shine forever.

Drums roll without pause in the caverned cities.
Swarms of flies want to feed
on white bread and black lips
and children in the manger.

If only the field's light would pierce the caves,
the poppies could smoke in the lamps,
pain consume them while they sleep,
until their burning was done.

Donkeys rise to carry water over the land.
All hands embroider lace,
glass and pearls for the walls,
a door in the ringing raiment.

Madonnas nurse children, buffalo pass
on their way to green refreshment.
Snake eggs, fish and the blood of lamb—
finally the gifts would suffice.

Stones grind fruit and the vessels at last are burned.
Oil streams down from an open eye,
poppies sink drunken to the earth,
trodden by tarantulas until they die.

Schatten Rosen Schatten

Unter einem fremden Himmel
Schatten Rosen
Schatten
auf einer fremden Erde
zwischen Rosen und Schatten
in einem fremden Wasser
mein Schatten

Shadow Roses Shadow

Beneath a foreign sky
shadow roses
shadow
on a foreign earth
between roses and shadows
in a foreign water
my shadow

Bleib

Die Fahrten gehn zu Ende,
der Fahrtenwind bleibt aus.
Es fällt dir in die Hände
ein leichtes Kartenhaus.

Die Karten sind bebildert
und zeigen jeden Ort.
Du hast die Welt geschildert
und mischst sie mit dem Wort.

Profundum der Partien,
die dann im Gange sind!
Bleib, um das Blatt zu ziehen,
mit dem man sie gewinnt.

Stay

The boats have all touched sand,
the fair wind heeds no call.
And lightly in your hand.
you see a card house fall.

Each card reveals a place
that you have once encountered.
You hold the world's face
and shuffle it with your word.

Oh infinite the joker's face
in card games big and small!
Stay, and draw the ace
with which to win them all.

An die Sonne

Schöner als der beachtliche Mond und sein geadeltes Licht,
Schöner als die Sterne, die berühmten Orden der Nacht,
Viel schöner als der feurige Auftritt eines Kometen
Und zu weit Schönrem berufen als jedes andre Gestirn,
Weil dein und mein Leben jeden Tag an ihr hängt, ist die
 Sonne.

Schöne Sonne, die aufgeht, ihr Werk nicht vergessen hat
Und beendet, am schönsten im Sommer, wenn ein Tag
An den Küsten verdampft und ohne Kraft gespiegelt die
 Segel
Über dein Aug ziehn, bis du müde wirst und das letzte
 verkürzt.

Ohne die Sonne nimmt auch die Kunst wieder den
 Schleier,
Du erscheinst mir nicht mehr, und die See und der Sand,
Von Schatten gepeitscht, fliehen unter mein Lid.

Schönes Licht, das uns warm hält, bewahrt und wunderbar
 sorgt,
Daß ich wieder sehe und daß ich dich wiederseh!

Nichts Schönres unter der Sonne als unter der Sonne zu
 sein...

Nichts Schönres als den Stab im Wasser zu sehn und den
 Vogel oben,
Der seinen Flug überlegt, und unten die Fische im
 Schwarm,

To the Sun

More beautiful than the venerable moon and her noble light,
More beautiful than the stars, the famous orders of night,
Much more beautiful than the fiery comet burst,
And called to more beauty than any heavenly body,
Since your life and my life depend on it daily, is the sun.

Beautiful sun that rises, remembers his chores
And finishes them, fairest in summer when a day
Steams off the coasts, and mirrored effortlessly the sails
Glide over your eye, till you grow tired and cut short the last.

Without the sun even art puts its veil back on,
You no longer appear to me, and the sea and the sand,
Whipped by shadows, take refuge under my eyelids.

Beautiful light that keeps us warm, sustains and cares for us
   wonderfully,
Letting me see again and see you again!

Nothing more beautiful under the sun than to be under the sun . . .

Nothing more beautiful than to see the rod in water and
   the bird above,
Pondering his flight, and down below the fish in their school.

Gefärbt, geformt, in die Welt gekommen mit einer
  Sendung von Licht,
Und den Umkreis zu sehn, das Geviert eines Felds, das
  Tausendeck meines Lands
Und das Kleid, das du angetan hast. Und dein Kleid,
  glockig und blau!

Schönes Blau, in dem die Pfauen spazieren und sich
  verneigen,
Blau der Fernen, der Zonen des Glücks mit den Wettern
  für mein Gefühl,
Blauer Zufall am Horizont! Und meine begeisterten Augen
Weiten sich wieder und blinken und brennen sich wund.

Schöne Sonne, der vom Staub noch die größte Bewunderung
  gebührt,
Drum werde ich nicht wegen dem Mond und den Sternen
  und nicht,
Weil die Nacht mit Kometen prahlt und in mir einen
  Narren sucht,
Sondern deinetwegen und bald endlos und wie um
  nichts sonst
Klage führen über den unabwendbaren Verlust
  meiner Augen.

Colored, shaped, come into the world with a mission of light,
And to see the radius, the square of a field, the geometry
   of my land
And the dress you put on. And your dress, billowing and blue.

Beautiful blue, in which peacocks stroll and bow,
Blue of distant skies, happy zones with weather for all my
   moods,
Blue chance on the horizon! And my zealous eyes
Open wide and blink and burn themselves sore.

Beautiful sun, which even the dust admires infinitely,
Hence not for the moon or the stars and not
Because the night shows off her comets and tries to fool me,
But for your sake and soon endlessly and as if nothing else
   mattered
I shall lament the unavoidable loss of my eyes.

Lieder auf der Flucht

Dura legge d'Amor! ma, ben che obliqua,
Servar convensi; però ch'ella aggiunge
Di cielo in terra, universale, antiqua.
                    Petrarca, ›I Trionfi‹

I

Der Palmzweig bricht im Schnee,
die Stiegen stürzen ein,
die Stadt liegt steif und glänzt
im fremden Winterschein.

Die Kinder schreien und ziehn
den Hungerberg hinan,
sie essen vom weißen Mehl
und beten den Himmel an.

Der reiche Winterflitter,
das Mandarinengold,
treibt in den wilden Böen.
Die Blutorange rollt.

II

Ich aber liege allein
im Eisverhau voller Wunden.

Es hat mir der Schnee
noch nicht die Augen verbunden.

Die Toten, an mich gepreßt,
schweigen in allen Zungen.

Songs of Flight

Dura legge d'Amor! ma, ben che obliqua,
Servar convensi; pero ch'ella aggiunge
Di cielo in terra, universale, antiqua.
                    Petrarca, "I Trionfi"

I

The palm frond breaks in snow,
the stairs are falling in.
The city lies stiff and gleams
in a strange winter glow.

The children utter cries
and climb the hunger mountain.
They eat from white flour
and worship the skies.

The rich winter tinsel,
the mandarin gold,
whirls in the wild squalls.
The blood orange rolls.

II

But I lie alone
in barbed ice covered with wounds.

Snow has not yet
bound my eyes.

The dead, pressed against me,
are silent in all tongues.

Niemand liebt mich und hat
für mich eine Lampe geschwungen!

III

Die Sporaden, die Inseln,
das schöne Stückwerk im Meer,
umschwommen von kalten Strömen,
neigen noch Früchte her.

Die weißen Retter, die Schiffe
– o einsame Segelhand! –
deuten, eh sie versinken,
zurück auf das Land.

IV

Kälte wie noch nie ist eingedrungen.
Fliegende Kommandos kamen über das Meer.
Mit allen Lichtern hat der Golf sich ergeben.
Die Stadt ist gefallen.

Ich bin unschuldig und gefangen
im unterworfenen Neapel,
wo der Winter
Posilip und Vomero an den Himmel stellt,
wo seine weißen Blitze aufräumen
unter den Liedern
und er seine heiseren Donner
ins Recht setzt.

Ich bin unschuldig, und bis Camaldoli
rühren die Pinien die Wolken;
und ohne Trost, denn die Palmen
schuppt sobald nicht der Regen;

No one loves me or has
swung a lamp for me!

III

The Sporades, the isles,
beautiful patchwork in the sea,
engulfed by cold streams
still bid fruit this way.

The white saviors, the ships
—oh lonely sailor hand!—
gesture, before they founder,
back toward the land.

IV

Unimaginable cold has broken in.
Flying commandos have covered the sea.
With all its lights the gulf has surrendered.
The city has fallen.

I am innocent and a captive
in conquered Naples,
where Winter
holds Posillipo and Vomero against the sky,
where his white lightning bolts ravage
among the songs
and he grants his hoarse thunder
its due.

I am innocent, and all the way to Camaldoli
the pine trees touch the clouds;
and without solace, for the rain
seldom sprinkles the palms.

ohne Hoffnung, denn ich soll nicht entkommen,
auch wenn der Fisch die Flossen schützend sträubt
und wenn am Winterstrand der Dunst,
von immer warmen Wellen aufgeworfen,
mir eine Mauer macht,
auch wenn die Wogen
fliehend
den Fliehenden
dem nächsten Ziel entheben.

V

Fort mit dem Schnee von der gewürzten Stadt!
Der Früchte Luft muß durch die Straßen gehen.
Streut die Korinthen aus,
die Feigen bringt, die Kapern!
Belebt den Sommer neu,
den Kreislauf neu,
Geburt, Blut, Kot und Auswurf,
Tod – hakt in die Striemen ein,
die Linien auferlegt
Gesichtern
mißtrauisch, faul und alt,
von Kalk umrissen und in Öl getränkt,
von Händeln schlau,
mit der Gefahr vertraut,
dem Zorn des Lavagotts,
dem Engel Rauch
und der verdammten Glut!

And without hope, for I shall not escape,
even when the fish ruffles its fins to protect me
or when haze on the winter beach,
risen from an ever warm surf,
builds me a wall,
or even when the waves,
fleeing,
free the fugitive
from his next goal.

V

Remove the snow from this spiced city!
Fruit air must waft through the streets.
Scatter the raisins,
bring in the figs, the capers!
Quicken the summer's step,
the cycle of the seasons.
Birth, blood, dung and phlegm,
death—catch hold of the welts,
the lines imposed on
faces
suspicious, lazy and old,
encircled with chalk and drenched in oil,
sly from quarreling,
intimate with danger
and the anger of the lava god,
with angel smoke
and cursed embers!

VI

Unterrichtet in der Liebe
durch zehntausend Bücher,
belehrt durch die Weitergabe
wenig veränderbarer Gesten
und törichter Schwüre –

eingeweiht in die Liebe
aber erst hier –
als die Lava herabfuhr
und ihr Hauch uns traf
am Fuß des Berges,
als zuletzt der erschöpfte Krater
den Schlüssel preisgab
für diese verschlossenen Körper –

Wir traten ein in verwunschene Räume
und leuchteten das Dunkel aus
mit den Fingerspitzen.

VII

Innen sind deine Augen Fenster
auf ein Land, in dem ich in Klarheit stehe.

Innen ist deine Brust ein Meer,
das mich auf den Grund zieht.
Innen ist deine Hüfte ein Landungssteg
für meine Schiffe, die heimkommen
von zu großen Fahrten.

Das Glück wirkt ein Silbertau,
an dem ich befestigt liege.

VI

Tutored in love
by ten thousand books,
wise from the tradition
of scarcely alterable gestures
and foolish oaths—

initiated into love
but only here—
when the lava bolted down
and its breath hit us
at the foot of the mountain,
when at last the exhausted crater
revealed the key
for these locked bodies—

We stepped into enchanted chambers
and lit the darkness away
with our fingertips.

VII

Within, your eyes are windows
on a land where I stand in clarity.

Within, your breast is a sea
that pulls me to its bed.
Within, your hip is a landing pier
for my ships, coming home
from too long a voyage.

Happiness twines a silver rope
to which I lie moored.

Innen ist dein Mund ein flaumiges Nest
für meine flügge werdende Zunge.
Innen ist dein Fleisch melonenlicht,
süß und genießbar ohne Ende.
Innen sind deine Adern ruhig
und ganz mit dem Gold gefüllt,
das ich mit meinen Tränen wasche
und das mich einmal aufwiegen wird.

Du empfängst Titel, deine Arme umfangen Güter,
die an dich zuerst vergeben werden.

Innen sind deine Füße nie unterwegs,
sondern schon angekommen in meinen Samtlanden.
Innen sind deine Knochen helle Flöten,
aus denen ich Töne zaubern kann,
die auch den Tod bestricken werden . . .

VIII

. . . Erde, Meer und Himmel.
Von Küssen zerwühlt
die Erde,
das Meer und der Himmel.
Von meinen Worten umklammert
die Erde,
von meinem letzten Wort noch umklammert
das Meer und der Himmel!

Heimgesucht von meinen Lauten
diese Erde,
die schluchzend in meinen Zähnen
vor Anker ging
mit allen ihren Hochöfen, Türmen
und hochmütigen Gipfeln,

Within, your mouth is a downy nest
for my fledgling tongue.
Within, your flesh is melon light,
sweet and delicious unendingly.
Within, your veins are calm
and filled with the gold
that I wash with my tears
and one day will outweigh me.

You receive titles, your arms embrace goods
that you are first to be granted.

Within, your feet are never travelling
but have already arrived in my velvet lands.
Within, your bones are bright flutes
from which I charm melodies
that enrapture even death . . .

VIII

. . . Earth, sea and sky.
Raked with kisses
the earth,
the sea and the sky.
Gripped by my words
the earth,
still held by my last word
the sea and the sky.

Haunted by my tones
this earth that,
sobbing in my teeth,
cast anchor
with all her blast furnaces, towers
and proud peaks.

diese geschlagene Erde,
die vor mir ihre Schluchten entblößte,
ihre Steppen, Wüsten und Tundren,

diese rastlose Erde
mit ihren zuckenden Magnetfeldern,
die sich hier selbst fesselte
mit ihr noch unbekannten Kraftketten,

diese betäubte und betäubende Erde
mit Nachtschattengewächsen,
bleiernen Giften
und Strömen von Duft –

untergegangen im Meer
und aufgegangen im Himmel
die Erde!

IX

Die schwarze Katze,
das Öl auf dem Boden,
der böse Blick:

Unglück!

Zieh das Korallenhorn,
häng die Hörner vors Haus,
Dunkel, kein Licht!

X

O Liebe, die unsre Schalen
aufbrach und fortwarf, unseren Schild,
den Wetterschutz und braunen Rost von Jahren!

This beaten earth
that bared her gorges to me,
her steppes, deserts and tundra;

this restless earth,
with quivering magnetic fields,
that fettered herself here
with her own unimagined chains of power.

This stunned and stunning earth
with nightshade flowers
lead poisons
and rivers of fragrance—

gone down in the sea
and risen in the sky
the earth!

IX

The black cat,
oil on the floor,
the evil look:

Trouble!

Take out the coral horn,
hang the horns before the house,
darkness, no light!

X

Oh love that broke open and cast away
our shells, our shield,
the weather guard and brown rust of many years!

O Leiden, die unsre Liebe austraten,
ihr feuchtes Feuer in den fühlenden Teilen!
Verqualmt, verendend im Qualm, geht die Flamme in sich.

XI

Du willst das Wetterleuchten, wirfst die Messer,
du trennst der Luft die warmen Adern auf;

dich blendend, springen aus den offnen Pulsen
lautlos die letzten Feuerwerke auf:

Wahnsinn, Verachtung, dann die Rache,
und schon die Reue und der Widerruf.

Du nimmst noch wahr, daß deine Klingen stumpfen,
und endlich fühlst du, wie die Liebe schließt:

mit ehrlichen Gewittern, reinem Atem.
Und sie verstößt dich in das Traumverlies.

Wo ihre goldnen Haare niederhängen,
greifst du nach ihr, der Leiter in das Nichts.

Tausend und eine Nacht hoch sind die Sprossen.
Der Schritt ins Leere ist der letzte Schritt.

Und wo du aufprallst, sind die alten Orte,
und jedem Ort gibst du drei Tropfen Blut.

Umnachtet hältst du wurzellose Locken.
Die Schelle läutet, und es ist genug.

Oh pain that stamped out our love,
its moist fire in tender places.
Smoke-filled, perishing in smoke, the flame turns in on itself.

XI

You want the summer lightning, and fling the knives,
you cut open the air's warm veins;

blinding you, from open wounds
the last fireworks shoot up in silence.

Madness, scorn, then revenge
and already remorse and the disavowal.

Yet still you feel your blades growing dull,
and finally you sense how love expires:

with honest storms, untainted breath.
And she casts you in the dream dungeon.

Where love's golden hair hangs down
you reach for her, for the ladder into nothing.

The rungs are a thousand and one nights high.
The step into emptiness is the last step.

And you hit bottom at the old places,
and to each you give three drops of blood.

Deranged, you hold rootless locks of hair.
The bell rings and you've had enough.

XII

Mund, der in meinem Mund genächtigt hat,
Aug, das mein Aug bewachte,
Hand –

und die mich schleiften, die Augen!
Mund, der das Urteil sprach,
Hand, die mich hinrichtete!

XIII

Die Sonne wärmt nicht, stimmlos ist das Meer.
Die Gräber, schneeverpackt, schnürt niemand auf.
Wird denn kein Kohlenbecken angefüllt
mit fester Glut? Doch Glut tut's nicht.

Erlöse mich! Ich kann nicht länger sterben.

Der Heilige hat anderes zu tun;
er sorgt sich um die Stadt und geht ums Brot.
Die Wäscheleine trägt so schwer am Tuch;
bald wird es fallen. Doch mich deckt's nicht zu.

Ich bin noch schuldig. Heb mich auf.
Ich bin nicht schuldig. Heb mich auf.

Das Eiskorn lös vom zugefrornen Aug,
brich mit den Blicken ein,
die blauen Gründe such,
schwimm, schau und tauch:

Ich bin es nicht.
Ich bin's.

XII

Mouth that has slept in mine,
eye that has watched over my eye,
hand—

and the eyes that bore through me!
Mouth that spoke the verdict,
hand that hung me!

XIII

The sun does not warm, voiceless is the sea.
No one unlocks the graves wrapped in snow.
Is no brazier being filled
with glowing embers? I feel no warmth.

Release me! I cannot die any longer.

The saint has other business;
he cares for the city and begs for bread.
The washline is laden with cloth.
Soon it will fall. But it will not cover me.

I am still guilty. Raise me.
I am not guilty. Raise me.

Free the ice from the frozen eye.
Break through with your glances,
seek the blue depths,
swim, look and dive.

It is not I.
It is I.

XIV

Wart meinen Tod ab und dann hör mich wieder,
es kippt der Schneekorb, und das Wasser singt,
in die Toledo münden alle Töne, es taut,
ein Wohlklang schmilzt das Eis.
O großes Tauen!

Erwart dir viel!

Silben im Oleander,
Wort im Akaziengrün
Kaskaden aus der Wand.

Die Becken füllt,
hell und bewegt,
Musik.

XV

Die Liebe hat einen Triumph und der Tod hat einen,
die Zeit und die Zeit danach.
Wir haben keinen.

Nur Sinken um uns von Gestirnen. Abglanz und Schweigen.
Doch das Lied überm Staub danach
wird uns übersteigen.

XIV

Wait for my death and then hear me again.
The snow basket tips over and the water sings,
all sounds merge into the Toledo, the ice is thawing.
A melody melts the ice.
Oh great thaw!

Ask much of yourself.

Syllables in oleander,
word in acacian green,
cascades from the wall.

Fill the basins,
bright and swaying,
music.

XV

Love has a triumph and death has one,
the time and the time thereafter.
We have none.

Only the sinking of stars about us. Reflected splendor and
    silence.
Yet the song above the dust
one day will rise above us.

SELECTED LATER POEMS

[Verordnet diesem Geschlecht keinen Glauben]

Verordnet diesem Geschlecht keinen Glauben,
genug sind Sterne, Schiffe und Rauch,
es legt sich in die Dinge, bestimmt
Sterne und die unendliche Zahl,
und ein Zug tritt, nenn ihn Zug einer Liebe,
reiner aus allem hervor.

Die Himmel hängen welk und Sterne lösen
sich aus der Verknüpfung mit Mond und Nacht.

[Don't prescribe any faith to this race]

Don't prescribe any faith to this race;
stars, ships and smoke will suffice.
The race engulfs all things, determines
stars and the infinite number,
and a trait, call it a trait of love,
emerges all the purer.

The skies hang wilted, and stars loose
themselves from the knot of moon and night.

Hôtel de la Paix

Die Rosenlast stürzt lautlos von den Wänden,
und durch den Teppich scheinen Grund und Boden.
Das Lichtherz bricht der Lampe.
Dunkel. Schritte.
Der Riegel hat sich vor den Tod geschoben.

Hôtel de la Paix

The burden of roses falls silent from the walls,
and through the rug shine floor and earth.
The heart of light breaks inside the lamp.
Darkness. Steps.
The bolt has been pushed before death.

Exil

Ein Toter bin ich der wandelt
gemeldet nirgends mehr
unbekannt im Reich des Präfekten
überzählig in den goldenen Städten
und im grünenden Land

abgetan lange schon
und mit nichts bedacht

Nur mit Wind mit Zeit und mit Klang

der ich unter Menschen nicht leben kann

Ich mit der deutschen Sprache
dieser Wolke um mich
die ich halte als Haus
treibe durch alle Sprachen

O wie sie sich verfinstert
die dunklen die Regentöne
nur die wenigen fallen

In hellere Zonen trägt dann sie den Toten hinauf

Exile

I am a dead man who wanders
registered nowhere
unknown in the realm of the prefect
superfluous in the golden cities
and the greening land

written off long ago
bequeathed nothing

Save wind and time and sound

I who cannot live among people

I with the German language
this cloud about me
that I keep as a house
drive through all languages

Oh how this cloud darkens
the somber ones the rain notes
only a few fall

Into brighter places it bears the dead man high

Nach dieser Sintflut

Nach dieser Sintflut
möchte ich die Taube,
und nichts als die Taube,
noch einmal gerettet sehn.

Ich ginge ja unter in diesem Meer!
flög' sie nicht aus,
brächte sie nicht
in letzter Stunde das Blatt.

After This Deluge

After this deluge
I would like to see the dove,
and nothing but the dove,
saved once more.

For I'd perish in this sea!
if she didn't fly away,
if she didn't bring back,
in the last hour,
the leaf.

Strömung

So weit im Leben und so nah am Tod,
daß ich mit niemand darum rechten kann,
reiß ich mir von der Erde meinen Teil;

dem stillen Ozean stoß ich den grünen Keil
mitten ins Herz und schwemm mich selber an.

Zinnvögel steigen auf und Zimtgeruch!
Mit meinem Mörder Zeit bin ich allein.
In Rausch und Bläue puppen wir uns ein.

Stream

So far in life and so close to death,
that I shall litigate no more.
From the earth I rip my part;

into the still ocean, into its heart
I plunge my green wedge and wash myself onshore.

Tin birds rise up and cinnamon smell!
With my murderer time I am alone.
In stupor, in blueness we spin our cocoon.

Geh, Gedanke

Geh, Gedanke, solang ein zum Flug klares Wort
dein Flügel ist, dich aufhebt und dorthin geht,
wo die leichten Metalle sich wiegen,
wo die Luft schneidend ist
in einem neuen Verstand,
wo Waffen sprechen
von einziger Art.
Verficht uns dort!

Die Woge trug ein Treibholz hoch und sinkt.
Das Fieber riß dich an sich, läßt dich fallen.
Der Glaube hat nur einen Berg versetzt.

Laß stehn, was steht, geh, Gedanke!,

von nichts andrem als unsrem Schmerz durchdrungen.
Entsprich uns ganz!

Go, My Thought

Go, my thought, as long as a word clear enough for flight
is your wing, lifts you and goes
where the light metals sway,
where the air is sharp
in a new understanding,
where weapons speak
of a single kind.
Defend us there!

The wave bore a piece of driftwood high and sinks.
Fever pulled you to its breast, lets you fall.
Faith has moved only a mountain.

Let stand what stands, go, my thought!

Filled with nothing other than our suffering.
Conform to us wholly!

Aria I

Wohin wir uns wenden im Gewitter der Rosen,
ist die Nacht von Dornen erhellt, und der Donner
des Laubs, das so leise war in den Büschen,
folgt uns jetzt auf dem Fuß.

Wo immer gelöscht wird, was die Rosen entzünden,
schwemmt Regen uns in den Fluß. O fernere Nacht!
Doch ein Blatt, das uns traf, treibt auf den Wellen
bis zur Mündung uns nach.

Aria I

Wherever we turn in the storm of roses,
thorns illuminate the night. And the thunder
of a thousand leaves, once so quiet on the bushes,
is right at our heels.

Wherever the roses' fire is put out,
rain washes us into the river. Oh distant night!
Yet a leaf that touched us now floats on the waves,
following us to the sea.

Ihr Worte

Für Nelly Sachs, die Freundin, die Dichterin, in Verehrung

Ihr Worte, auf, mir nach!,
und sind wir auch schon weiter,
zu weit gegangen, geht's noch einmal
weiter, zu keinem Ende geht's.

Es hellt nicht auf.

Das Wort
wird doch nur
andre Worte nach sich ziehn,
Satz den Satz.
So möchte Welt,
endgültig,
sich aufdrängen,
schon gesagt sein.
Sagt sie nicht.

Worte, mir nach,
daß nicht endgültig wird
– nicht diese Wortbegier
und Spruch auf Widerspruch!

Laßt eine Weile jetzt
keins der Gefühle sprechen,
den Muskel Herz
sich anders üben.

Laßt, sag ich, laßt.

You Words

For Nelly Sachs, poet and friend

You words, come, after me!
And though we've gone a long way,
too long, we must go
on, we'll never reach the end.

The sky isn't getting light.

The word
can only
pull other words behind it,
one sentence another.
So world would like,
finally,
to obtrude itself,
already be said.
Don't say it.

Words, after me,
so that this hunger for words,
statement and counterstatement
—does not become final.

For a while let
none of the senses speak,
let the muscle heart
exercise differently.

Let be, I say, let be.

Ins höchste Ohr nicht,
nichts, sag ich, geflüstert,
zum Tod fall dir nichts ein,
laß, und mir nach, nicht mild
noch bitterlich,
nicht trostreich,
ohne Trost
bezeichnend nicht,
so auch nicht zeichenlos –

Und nur nicht dies: das Bild
im Staubgespinst, leeres Geroll
von Silben, Sterbenswörter.

Kein Sterbenswort,
Ihr Worte!

Not into exalted ears,
nothing, I say, whispered,
no thoughts about death,
let be, and after me, not mild
nor bitterly,
not comforting
without consolation
not designating,
thus not without signs—

And above all not this: the image
in the web of dust, hollow roll
of syllables, last words.

No dying word,
you words!

Wahrlich

Für Anna Achmatova

Wem es ein Wort nie verschlagen hat,
und ich sage es euch,
wer bloß sich zu helfen weiß
und mit den Worten –

dem ist nicht zu helfen.
Über den kurzen Weg nicht
und nicht über den langen.

Einen einzigen Satz haltbar zu machen,
auszuhalten in dem Bimbam von Worten.

Es schreibt diesen Satz keiner,
der nicht unterschreibt.

Truly

For Anna Achmatova

Whoever has not choked on a word,
and I say unto you,
whoever knows merely how to help himself,
and with words—

there's no helping him.
Not in the short run
and not in the long one.

To make a single sentence tenable,
to endure it in the ding-dong of words.

No one writes this sentence
who doesn't under-write.

Böhmen liegt am Meer

Sind hierorts Häuser grün, tret ich noch in ein Haus.
Sind hier die Brücken heil, geh ich auf gutem Grund.
Ist Liebesmüh in alle Zeit verloren, verlier ich sie hier gern.

Bin ich's nicht, ist es einer, der ist so gut wie ich.

Grenzt hier ein Wort an mich, so laß ich's grenzen.
Liegt Böhmen noch am Meer, glaub ich den Meeren
  wieder.
Und glaub ich noch ans Meer, so hoffe ich auf Land.

Bin ich's, so ist's ein jeder, der ist soviel wie ich.
Ich will nichts mehr für mich. Ich will zugrunde gehn.

Zugrund – das heißt zum Meer, dort find ich Böhmen
  wieder.
Zugrund gerichtet, wach ich ruhig auf.
Von Grund auf weiß ich jetzt, und ich bin unverloren.

Kommt her, ihr Böhmen alle, Seefahrer, Hafenhuren und
  Schiffe
unverankert. Wollt ihr nicht böhmisch sein, Illyrer,
  Veroneser,
und Venezianer alle. Spielt die Komödien, die lachen
  machen

Und die zum Weinen sind. Und irrt euch hundertmal,
wie ich mich irrte und Proben nie bestand,
doch hab ich sie bestanden, ein um das andre Mal.

Wie Böhmen sie bestand und eines schönen Tags
ans Meer begnadigt wurde und jetzt am Wasser liegt.

Bohemia Lies by the Sea

If the houses here are green, I'll step inside a house.
If the bridges here are strong, I'll walk on solid ground.
If love's labor is lost in every age, I'd like to lose it here.

If I'm not the one, someone is, he's just as good as I.

If a word borders on me here, I'll let it border.
If Bohemia still lies by the sea, I'll believe in the sea.
And if I believe in the sea, I can hope for land.

If I'm the one, then anyone is, he's worth as much as I.
I want nothing more for myself. Let me go under now.

Underground—that means the ocean, there I'll find Bohemia
    again.
From my ruins, I wake up in peace.
From deep down I know, and am not lost.

Come here, all you Bohemians, seamen, harbor whores and
    ships
unanchored. Don't you want to be Bohemians, all you Illyrians,
Venetians and Veronese. Play the comedies that make us laugh

to tears. And go astray a hundred times,
as I went astray and never stood the trials.
Yet I did stand them, each and every time.

As Bohemia stood them and one fine day
was pardoned to the sea and now lies by water.

Ich grenz noch an ein Wort und an ein andres Land,
ich grenz, wie wenig auch, an alles immer mehr,

ein Böhme, ein Vagant, der nichts hat, den nichts hält,
begabt nur noch, vom Meer, das strittig ist, Land meiner
 Wahl zu sehen.

I still border on a word and a different land,
I border, like little else, on everything more and more,

a man from Bohemia, a vagrant, a player
who has nothing and whom nothing holds,
granted only, by a questionable sea, to gaze at the land of my choice.

Prag Jänner 64

Seit jener Nacht
gehe und spreche ich wieder,
böhmisch klingt es,
als wär ich wieder zuhause,

wo zwischen der Moldau, der Donau
und meinem Kindheitsfluß
alles einen Begriff von mir hat.

Gehen, schrittweis ist es wiedergekommen,
Sehen, angeblickt, habe ich wieder erlernt.

Gebückt noch, blinzelnd,
hing ich am Fenster,
sah die Schattenjahre,
in denen kein Stern
mir in den Mund hing,
sich über den Hügel entfernen.

Über den Hradschin
haben um sechs Uhr morgens
die Schneeschaufler aus der Tatra
mit ihren rissigen Pranken
die Scherben dieser Eisdecke gekehrt.

Unter den berstenden Blöcken
meines, auch meines Flusses
kam das befreite Wasser hervor.

Zu hören bis zum Ural.

Prague January 64

Since that night
I walk and speak once more.
There's a Bohemian ring to words,
as if I were home again—

where between the Moldau, the Danube
and the river of my childhood
everything has a notion of me.

Going, it's come back step by step;
seeing, gazed upon, I've learned again.

Still bent over, squinting,
I hung by the window
and watched the shadow years,
in which no star
hung in my mouth,
disappear over the hill.

Above the Hradschin,
at six in the morning,
the snow shovelers from Tatry
with their calloused claws
have swept away the pieces of this ice blanket.

Beneath the bursting blocks
of my, yes also my river,
the freed water came forth.

Audible all the way to the Urals.

Eine Art Verlust

Gemeinsam benutzt: Jahreszeiten, Bücher und eine Musik.
Die Schlüssel, die Teeschalen, den Brotkorb, Leintücher
  und ein Bett.
Eine Aussteuer von Worten, von Gesten, mitgebracht,
  verwendet, verbraucht.
Eine Hausordnung beachtet. Gesagt. Getan. Und immer
  die Hand gereicht.

In Winter, in ein Wiener Septett und in Sommer habe ich
  mich verliebt.
In Landkarten, in ein Bergnest, in einen Strand und in
  ein Bett.
Einen Kult getrieben mit Daten, Versprechen für
  unkündbar erklärt,
angehimmelt ein Etwas und fromm gewesen vor einem
  Nichts,

(– der gefalteten Zeitung, der kalten Asche, dem Zettel
  mit einer Notiz)
furchtlos in der Religion, denn die Kirche war dieses Bett.

Aus dem Seeblick hervor ging meine unerschöpfliche
  Malerei.
Von dem Balkon herab waren die Völker, meine Nachbarn,
  zu grüßen.
Am Kaminfeuer, in der Sicherheit, hatte mein Haar seine
  äußerste Farbe.
Das Klingeln an der Tür war der Alarm für meine Freude.

Nicht dich habe ich verloren,
sondern die Welt.

A Kind of Loss

Used together: seasons, books, a piece of music.
The keys, teacups, bread basket, sheets and a bed.
A hope chest of words, of gestures, brought back, used, used up.
A household order maintained. Said. Done. And always a hand
 was there.

I've fallen in love with winter, with a Viennese septet, with
 summer.
With village maps, a mountain nest, a beach and a bed.
Kept a calender cult, declared promises irrevocable,
bowed before something, was pious to a nothing

(—to a folded newspaper, cold ashes, the scribbled piece of
 paper),
fearless in religion, for our bed was the church.

From my lake view arose my inexhaustible painting.
From my balcony I greeted entire peoples, my neighbors.
By the chimney fire, in safety, my hair took on its deepest hue.
The ringing at the door was the alarm for my joy.

It's not you I've lost,
but the world.

Enigma

Für Hans Werner Henze aus der Zeit der Ariosi

Nichts mehr wird kommen.

Frühling wird nicht mehr werden.
Tausendjährige Kalender sagen es jedem voraus.

Aber auch Sommer und weiterhin, was so gute Namen
wie »sommerlich« hat –
es wird nichts mehr kommen.

Du sollst ja nicht weinen,
sagt eine Musik.

Sonst
sagt
niemand
etwas.

Enigma
For Hans Werner Henze from the time of the Ariosi

Nothing more will come.

Spring will never be again.
Millenial calenders predict it to everyone.

But summer too, and more, everything with good names
like "summery"—
nothing more will come.

You shouldn't cry
the music says.

Otherwise
no one
says
anything.

Keine Delikatessen

Nichts mehr gefällt mir.

Soll ich
eine Metapher ausstaffieren
mit einer Mandelblüte?
die Syntax kreuzigen
auf einen Lichteffekt?
Wer wird sich den Schädel zerbrechen
über so überflüssige Dinge –

Ich habe ein Einsehn gelernt
mit den Worten,
die da sind
(für die unterste Klasse)

Hunger
        Schande
                Tränen
und
                      Finsternis.

Mit dem ungereinigten Schluchzen,
mit der Verzweiflung
(und ich verzweifle noch vor Verzweiflung)
über das viele Elend,
den Krankenstand, die Lebenskosten,
werde ich auskommen.

Ich vernachlässige nicht die Schrift,
sondern mich.
Die andern wissen sich
weißgott
mit den Worten zu helfen.
Ich bin nicht mein Assistent.

No Delicacies

Nothing pleases me anymore.

Should I
dress a metaphor
with an almond blossom?
crucify syntax
on a trick of light?
Who will beat his brains
over such superfluities—

I have learned to be considerate
with the words
that exist
(for the lowest class)

hunger
         disgrace
                  tears
and
                         darkness

With unclean sobbing,
with despair
(and I despair even of despair)
of the enormous misery,
the bedridden, the cost of living—
I will get by.

I don't neglect the word
but myself.
The others know
godknows
how to help themselves with words.
I am not my assistant.

Soll ich
einen Gedanken gefangennehmen,
abführen in eine erleuchtete Satzzelle?
Aug und Ohr verköstigen
mit Worthappen erster Güte?
erforschen die Libido eines Vokals,
ermitteln die Liebhaberwerte unserer Konsonanten?

Muß ich
mit dem verhagelten Kopf,
mit dem Schreibkrampf in dieser Hand,
unter dreihundertnächtigem Druck
einreißen das Papier,
wegfegen die angezettelten Wortopern,
vernichtend so: ich du und er sie es

wir ihr?

(Soll doch. Sollen die andern.)

Mein Teil, es soll verloren gehen.

Should I
take a thought captive,
lead it into an illuminated sentence cell?
Feed eye and ear
with first-class word tidbits?
Investigate the libido of a vowel,
ascertain the lover's value of our consonants?

Must I,
with this hail-battered head,
with writing cramps in this hand,
under the pressure of three hundred nights,
rip this paper apart,
sweep away the plotted word operas,
destroying thus: I you and he she it

we you?

(Still should. The others should.)

My share, it should be dispersed.

APPENDIX

Biographical Note*

I GREW UP in Carinthia,** near the border, in a valley that has two names—a German one and a Slovenian one. And the house inhabited for generations by my ancestors—Austrians and Wends—still bears a foreign-sounding name. So near the border is yet another border: the border of language. I felt at home here and on the other side, with the tales of good and evil spirits from two and three countries. For behind the mountains, just an hour away, is Italy.

I think the narrowness of this valley and the consciousness of borders have imparted to me a longing for distant places. When the war ended I left my home and, full of impatience and expectations, went to Vienna, which in my imagination had seemed unreachable. It became another home on the border: between East and West, between a long, noble past and a gloomy future. And if, later, I also traveled to Paris and London, Germany and Italy, that means little; for in my memory the road from my valley to Vienna will always be the longest.

Sometimes people ask me how I, who was raised in the country, found my way to literature. I'm not sure of the precise reason. I only know that at the age when children read Grimms' fairytales I began to write, and that I liked to lie beside the railroad embankment and send my thoughts on journeys to foreign cities and countries and to that unknown sea which, somewhere, merges with the sky to complete the globe. It was always of seas, sand, and ships that I dreamed. But then the war came, and the dream-filled, fantastic world of my youth was pushed out of the way by the real world where decisions, not dreams, come first.

---

* Translator's Note: Written sometime between May and September 1952 for a radio broadcast, this untitled autobiographical sketch was found among Bachmann's papers at her death.

** A province of southeastern Austria. (Tr)

Afterwards so much happened that one could scarcely wish for more: study at the university, travel, writing for magazines and newspapers, and later my constant work for a radio station. These everyday stations in a life may be rearranged and exchanged, one for the other. Yet life itself does not rely on such mediation.

There still remains the question of influence and models, of the literary climate in which one feels at home. For several years I consistently read a great deal. Among the more recent poets perhaps Gide, Valéry, Eluard, and Yeats were my favorites. And it may be that I learned much from them. But at heart I am still dominated by the mythic imaginative world of my home country, which is a facet of Austria yet to be realized—a world of many languages and many borders.

To write poetry seems to me the most difficult task because the problems of form, theme, and diction must be resolved into a single entity; and because poetry must obey the rhythm of the age and still bring into harmony the wealth of old and new things for our hearts, in which past, present, and future are enclosed.

What I Saw and Heard in Rome*

IN ROME I saw that the Tiber is not beautiful, but that it flows untroubled between quays and banks that no one dares disturb. No one uses the rust-brown freighters or the fishing boats. Bushes and high grass are covered with dirt, and the workers sleep on the stone railings, immobile in the noonday heat. Never has one rolled over. Never has one fallen. They sleep where plane trees offer them shade, and pull the sky over their heads. But the river's water is beautiful, muddy green or blond, depending on how the light falls. One should walk alongside the Tiber rather than look at it from the bridges, which are considered paths to an island. The Tiberina is inhabited by *noantri*—we others, a word that can be explained in the following way: the Tiberina, since antiquity the island of the sick and the dead, wishes to be inhabited by "us others," sailed by us, for she is also a ship and floats slowly in the water with all her passengers, in a river for which she is no burden.

In Rome I saw that St. Peter's appears smaller than its size and yet is still too big. It is said that God wanted his church to stand firm on a rock. But this one lifts itself over the grave of its saint, which now lies open. So it is the saint himself who endangers and weakens the church. Still the great festivals take place with all their fanfare, purple ballets are performed under baldaquins, and gold has replaced the wax in the niches. *Chiesa granne divozzione poca.* The poor, in their watchfulness, still make sure that the church doesn't fall; and the one who founded it is already counting on the tread of angels.

In Rome I saw that many houses resemble the Palazzo Cenci, in which unhappy Beatrice lived before her execution. The prices are high and the traces of barbarism everywhere.

* First published in *Akzente. Zeitschrift für Dichtung*, February 1955. (Tr)

The oleander containers on the balconies rot for the sake of white and red blossoms. The flowers would like to fly away, for they can't compete with the smell of excrement and decay, which, more than the monuments, brings the past to life.

In Rome I saw in the ghetto that you shouldn't count your chickens before they're hatched. But on Yom Kippur everyone is forgiven in advance for an entire year. Close to the synagogue a table has been set up in a *trattoria*, and there the small reddish fish from the Mediterranean are served, spiced with raisins and pine nuts. The old people recall their friends, whose weight was measured in gold, and that when they paid the ransom the transport wagons still drove up and no one came back. But their grandchildren, two small girls in fiery red dresses and a fat blond boy, dance between the tables and can't keep their eyes off the musicians. "Keep on playing," cries the fat one and waves his cap. His grandmother begins to smile, and the violinist goes white as a sheet and stops playing for a whole measure.

On the Campo de Fiori I saw that Giordano Bruno is still burned at the stake. Every Saturday evening when the stands around him are torn down and only the flower ladies are left, when the stench of fish, chlorine, and rotten fruit on the square ebbs away, the men carry the leftover garbage (everything's been rummaged through), put it in a heap before his eyes and ignite it. Smoke rises up once more and the flames twist in the air. A woman cries out and the others start shouting too. Because the flames are transparent in the intense light, one can't see how far they reach and what they're hitting at. But the man on the pedestal knows and still he doesn't recant.

In a Roman bar I saw and counted: a cat with funny ears and an almost naked face, white trousers and a honey-colored vest that's seen better days; a waiter who spilled coffee and let the aperitif glasses overflow; a small boy with an apron who washed cups and glasses and never went to bed before midnight; customers who came and went, and one customer who always came back and lived from a little swig of bitterness.

In Rome I've seen the great villas with real pine trees, cedar, and even beech carved into make-believe animals. At the Capitol I saw the laurel tree and the treacherous wild grass of the Forum. And at dusk, when the grass started attacking the broken pillars and crumbling walls, I heard the noise of the city, deceivingly distant, and the soft gliding of the cars.

I saw, in the place where Rome's streets sally forth, how the triumphant sky marched into the city, refused to bow under any gate and stretched itself out over the seven hills, blue after pirate raids along the coasts of Sicily and filled with the island fruits of the Tyrrhenian sea, unharmed after forays into the land of Abruzzian brigands and black with the swallow-grapes rescued over the Appenines. I saw the promised sky of ermine and the wretched sky of sackcloth, and I saw a steady hand in great moments inscribe the medial line above the rooftops.

That everyone builds his own house as he likes, I have often seen, and that no blueprint joins one to the other better than chance and individual taste. But no taste is enough to create the proper intervals, lonely fields for sun and shade. And no chance solves the equation in which the weight of a wall expresses the weightlessness of a tower. The houses are covered with old canvas, its colors dried out. Only when sunlight forces its way into the porous material does the color we see appear: a shade of brown capable of every metamorphosis.

In Rome I saw that everything has a name and that one must know the names. Even things wish to be named. The Ludovisian throne hasn't fallen with the last ruler. Columns from the temple of Venus remain standing—from this temple and no other. The head of Saint Agnes has shrunk but it hasn't become that of a leather doll. Like so many Popes before him, this Pope is carried in a sedan chair, and his blessing is good *urbis et orbi*. The noble families are called: Corsini and Pignatelli, Ruspoli and Odescalchi, Farnese and Barberini, Aldobrandini. . . . Those are still their names, even when the homeless set up their iron beds in a castle in the *campagna* or pile up their water containers on sarcophaguses. The last member of the family has long since moved away. In the city his rooms are marked with black brocade and he plays blue-blooded songs on a black piano. He cowers when he hears his name. So different from the animal that, rather than eat, provided nourishment from its own flesh for future generations: the she-wolf.

I saw that whoever said "Rome" still names the world, and that the key to strength is four letters. S.P.Q.R. Whoever knows the code can close the books. He can read it from the coat of arms on passing buses or a manhole cover. It's the identity card of the fountains and the dutied drinks; the sign of the only majesty that has ruled the city without interruption.

At the railway station, Termini, I saw that in Rome people say farewells more easily than elsewhere. For those departing leave their friends behind with a baggage claim-ticket to longing. The station is bordered by the remains of the Diocletian Wall, and inscribed on the new floating glass façade, three cypresses appear in an unmistakable script. For the classical form is the simplest, and old and new texts represent it equally well.

Whoever throws a coin in the Fontana di Trevi and wishes to come back fears it might not be accepted. But he can be consoled. At night a young boy sits on the edge of the fountain and whistles, luring the others out of hiding. When all have gathered the boy undresses and climbs nonchalantly into the water. Moonlight illuminates the scene while he bends over, shivering, to collect the coins. Finally he whistles again, and in his hands all currencies melt into silver. The booty can't be divided beneath the moon, for the boy has the appearance of a god in comparison with the others, whose forms are made of cheap coats and trousers.

It is hard to see what lies under the earth: water regions and cemeteries. Steps lead down to cisterns drunk dry by the wind, to fountains arched over with corbels and hollowed out of white tuff, and to drops of blood that have grown into springs. The paths sink into the catacombs. A match is struck and its flame expands into symbols. For a moment we see: fish, peacock and dove, anchor and cross, food and drink. The match goes out quickly and those walking ahead rush upstairs. In the curve someone stops short and asks: "Where is the wind coming from?"

When I lost my hearing and sight in Rome the sirocco came and defeated the eagle wind from the mountains. Then the sun wore a shirt and shone in a false light. In such times all misfortune increases and a harsh word is easily spoken. For the warm wind reaches back to the desert. Sometimes it announces its arrival, scatters red sand over the groggy city, and blows on it until it is senseless. When the sirocco blows, it does so secretly, in the middle of the night, while we sleep obliviously. But in the morning, around three, dew falls. How I envy the one who could lie there awake and wet his lips!

In the morning in Rome I've looked across the Protestant graveyard to the Testaccio and thrown my sorrow in with the rest. Whoever digs up a little earth will find the sorrow of others below. For the graveyard seeking shade along the Aurelian Wall, the shards on the Testaccio are not counted but few. It holds a great cloud next to its ear like a conch and now hears only one sound. In it are the words: "One whose name was writ in water,"* and next to Keats's verses a handful of lines by Shelley. Not a word of Humboldt's little son who died of malaria. And of August von Goethe not a word either. Of the mute painters, Karstens and Marées, a few lines have survived, a spot of color, a knowing blue. Of the other mute ones, nobody has ever known.

In Rome, of course, I have heard that many have bread to

---

* In English in the original text. (Tr)

eat but not the teeth, and that the flies must bite into thin horses. That one is given many gifts and the other none, that whoever pulls too hard will rip something, and that only a solid pillar holds up a house for a hundred years. I have heard that in the world there is more time than understanding, but that we were given our eyes to see.

[On the Origin of the Title "In Apulia"]*
[Sketch]

ONE SELDOM speaks of a poem's title. How does the poet decide on a title? Does he start out with the title or look for it afterwards? What happens when he can't find one? I believe that all poets—and not just poets—have found themselves at a loss over this problem. Recently poets have preferred to extract a line from the poem in question, a line in which the poem appears to culminate; but they shouldn't be surprised if the reader takes hold of this one line and forgets the others.

With my poem "In Apulia" the title suggested itself; there was a reason for naming it thus. Someone to whom I had given the poem to read asked: "You were in Apulia? Where is that anyway?—Oh, I see." Apulia can be found on an Italian map. It is one of Italy's lesser known regions, an old land, a part of Magna Graecia, a highway for the Lombards, diffuse in its expressions, sandstone Baroque in Lecce, Gothic in Trani and Bari, Greek churches in Galipoli, nowadays overgrown and bathed only in light, a land of peasants and small ports, of *frutti di mare*, oyster stands in Taranto. The Germans have rarely made it down there . . . the classical Italian roads don't lead there.

Of course I was in Apulia; but "In Apulia" is something different. It dissolves the land into landscape and leads the landscape back to the land. There are wonderfully beautiful names for the primeval lands, dreamt or sunk into the sea, Atlantis and Orplid. "Apulia" is a beautiful name—I don't think anybody could bring himself to say "Le Puglie," for Italian doesn't convey it, being merely geographical. And anyway, how

---

* This untitled fragment, which was found among Bachmann's papers after her death, breaks off with the following words: "So let us concentrate on the poem itself. It has five stanzas. The first leads us to Apulia. The source of light is identified. The first two stanzas. . . ." (Tr)

strange it is to say "in France" or "in Sweden," as if we were speaking of containers and their contents.

I'm not sure whether it was in Apulia or Lucania that I looked out of the train window into an olive grove and saw a huge carpet of poppies stretching all the way to the horizon. In such a moment one lights a cigarette or flattens oneself against the corridor wall to let somebody by. But perhaps it wasn't that unnoticed moment but the one in which "In Apulia" was written. The process consists of many factors, of writing, of thinking with a growing concentration that flows back into the writing. The water into which a river flows doesn't remember its sources, its tributaries, the banks it touched, the grass it surged over or the roots and stems it ripped along in its course.

There are many precise images for production that suggest themselves, on the path from process to form; but only one precise image for process and form. And that image coincides with the poem itself. . . .

[What Good Are Poems?]*

TO ASK a playwright or a novelist what his favorite work is will not disturb him. He will no doubt remember one or two that have brought joy to some individuals, or understanding or pleasure—even if only for a few hours. I have never heard of someone spending a fruitful afternoon or an evening with a poem, although undoubtedly lovers of poetry still exist, as well as those who find in it a means of edification. And then there are the children who must learn poetry by heart, for poems—so it is said—sharpen our memory.

There is, then, little happiness in a poem. For the writer, the fact that it is a successful poem or may reach someone brings no happiness. The poem is lonely; it has no function and rightly concerns no one. A poem nowadays no longer exalts anything, and even the believers have long since rescinded its powers. Fame and belief reside within the poem itself.

In recent times one often hears (the profanation of) Hölderlin's question: "And what good are poets in a needy age?" Another question, just as valid, might be: "And what good are poems?" What is to be proved and for whom must it be proved? If poems supposedly prove nothing, then we must content ourselves with the notion that they sharpen our memory.

I believe poems can do just this. And that whoever writes poetry engraves forms in our memory, wonderful old words for stone or leaf, tied to or released by new words, new signs of reality. And I believe that whoever inscribes these forms also disappears into them with his own breath, which he offers as the unrequested proof of these forms' truth.

How long has it been that someone said to us: "Make a

* First published in *Monatshefte*, April 1955, for a column entitled "My Favorite Poem" that included poems and commentaries by Ingeborg Bachmann, Rudolf Hagelstange, Karl Krolow, and Heinz Piontek. Bachmann chose "The Heavy Freight." (Tr)

word, make a sentence!" We were tormented with poems; and the welts still sting in our memory. One of these poems began: "I stood on my land's borders. . . ." Who, and what land was it about? What the borders meant could of course be determined by the context. For whoever accepts the rules and enters the game won't throw the ball out of the playing field. The playing field is language, and its borders are the borders of the world—a world gazed on without question, nakedly and precisely imagined, experienced in pain, and in happiness celebrated and praised.

The Poem for the Reader*
[Sketch]

WHATEVER separated us? If I look at myself in the mirror and ask that question, I see myself backwards, a lonely piece of writing, and I no longer understand myself. In this tremendously cold age we should have coldly turned away from each other despite our unquenchable love? I tossed you smoking words, burned, with a bitter taste, cutting sentences or dull ones without luster. As if I wished to increase your misery and banish you from my territories with my intellect. You came so trustingly, sometimes awkwardly, asking for a word with beautiful colors. You wanted to be consoled and I had no consolation to give. Profundity is not my business either.

But an unquenchable love for you has never left me, and now I am searching under the rubble and in the air, in the ice-wind and the sun, for the words that should throw me back into your arms. For I am consumed with longing for you.

I'm not a piece of fabric, I'm not made of a cloth that could cover your nakedness, but of the fusion of all materials. And I want to burst into your senses and your mind like gold veins in the earth, illuminate and shine through you when the black fire, your mortality, starts burning inside you.

I don't know what you want of me. I can't write the song that would accompany you into victorious battle. I retreat before the altars. I am not your go-between. All your business deals leave me cold. But not you. Only not you.

You are everything to me. What wouldn't I want to be for you. I'd like to follow you when you're dead, look back to see you even if I might be turned into stone. I'd like to ring with song, move the remaining beasts to tears, make the stones bloom, draw fragrance from every bough.

* Of uncertain date. (Tr)

Chronology

1926	Birth on June 25 in Klagenfurt, a small city in southeastern Austria near the Yugoslavian and Italian borders.
1945-50	University study in Innsbruck, Graz, and Vienna, at first in law and philosophy, later exclusively in philosophy.
1950	Degree awarded by the University of Vienna for a dissertation entitled *The Critical Reception of Martin Heideggers's Existential Philosophy*.
1951-53	Scriptwriter for the radio group Rot/Weiss/Rot in Vienna.
1952	First reading for the literary group "47" in Niendorf. Libretto for the ballet *The Idiot* by Tatjana Gsovsky, music by Hans Werner Henze.
1953	*Mortgaged Time*, poetry, published by the Frankfurt Verlagsanstalt. Group 47 prize. "Ludwig Wittgenstein: A Chapter in the Recent History of German Philosophy," essay.
1953-57	Residence in Italy on the island of Ischia, in Naples, and in Rome.
1954	*The Cicadas*, radio play.
1955	"What I Saw and Heard in Rome," essay. Literary prize of the Cultural Circle of German Industry. Travel to the United States on the invitation of Henry Kissinger and Harvard University.
1956	*Invocation of the Great Bear*, poetry, published by Piper, Munich.
1957	Literature Prize from the city of Bremen.
1957-58	Residence in Munich.
1958	*The Good God of Manhattan*, radio play.

1958-73	Residence in Zurich and Rome, later primarily in Rome.
1959	Radio play prize from the War Blind for *The Good God of Manhattan*.
1959-60	First lecturer to occupy the newly created chair for poetry at the University of Frankfurt. Five lectures given under the title *Problems of Contemporary Poetry*.
1960	Libretto for Hans Werner Henze's opera *The Prince of Homburg*.
1961	*The Thirtieth Year*, stories, published by Piper, Munich. Berlin Critics' Prize for same. *Giuseppe Ungaretti: Gedichte*, poetry translation, published by Suhrkamp, Frankfurt.
1964	Georg Büchner Prize. *A Place for Chance*, essay and acceptance speech for Büchner Prize. Published by Klaus Wagenbach, Berlin, with thirteen drawings by Günter Grass.
1965	Libretto for *The Young Lord*, comic opera in two acts by Hans Werner Henze.
1968	Grand Austrian State Prize.
1971	*Malina*, novel, published by Suhrkamp, Frankfurt.
1972	*Simultaneous*, stories, published by Piper, Munich. Anton Wildgans Prize of Austrian Industry.
1973	Death in Rome on October 17.

The Lockert Library of Poetry in Translation

George Seferis: Collected Poems (1924-1955), translated, edited, and introduced by Edmund Keeley and Philip Sherrard

Collected Poems of Lucio Piccolo, translated and edited by Brian Swann and Ruth Feldman

C.P. Cavafy: Collected Poems, translated by Edmund Keeley and Philip Sherrard and edited by George Savidis

Benny Andersen: Selected Poems, translated by Alexander Taylor

Selected Poetry of Andrea Zanzotto, translated and edited by Ruth Feldman and Brian Swann

Poems of René Char, translated by Mary Ann Caws and Jonathan Griffin

Selected Poems of Tudor Arghezi, translated and edited by Michael Impey and Brian Swann

"The Survivor" and Other Poems by Tadeusz Różewicz, translated and introduced by Magnus J. Krynski and Robert A. Maguire

"Harsh World" and Other Poems by Ángel González, translated by Donald D. Walsh

Ritsos in Parentheses, translations and introduction by Edmund Keeley

Salamander: Selected Poems of Robert Marteau, translated by Anne Winters

Angelos Sikelianos: Selected Poems, translated and introduced by Edmund Keeley and Philip Sherrard

Dante's "Rime," translated by Patrick S. Diehl

Selected Later Poems of Marie Luise Kaschnitz, translated by Lisel Mueller

Osip Mandelstam's "Stone," translated and introduced by Robert Tracy

The Dawn Is Always New: Selected Poetry of Rocco Scotellaro, translated by Ruth Feldman and Brian Swann

Sounds, Feelings, Thoughts: Seventy Poems by Wisława Szymborska, translated and introduced by Magnus J. Krynski and Robert A. Maguire

The Man I Pretend to Be: "The Colloquies" and Selected Poems of Guido Gozzano, translated and edited by Michael Palma, with an introductory essay by Eugenio Montale

D'Après Tout: Poems by Jean Follain, translated by Heather McHugh

Songs of Something Else: Selected Poems of Gunnar Ekelöf, translated by Leonard Nathan and James Larson

The Little Treasury of One Hundred People, One Poem Each, compiled by Fujiwara No Sadaie and translated by Tom Galt

The Ellipse: Selected Poems of Leonardo Sinisgalli, translated by W. S. Di Piero

The Difficult Days by Roberto Sosa, translated by Jim Lindsey

Hymns and Fragments by Friedrich Hölderlin, translated and introduced by Richard Sieburth

Rilke: Between Roots, Selected Poems Rendered from the German by Rika Lesser

In the Storm of Roses: Selected Poems by Ingeborg Bachmann, translated, edited, and introduced by Mark Anderson

LIBRARY OF CONGRESS CATALOGING-IN-PUBLICATION DATA

Bachmann, Ingeborg, 1926-1973.
In the storm of roses.

(Lockert library of poetry in translation)
1. Bachmann, Ingeborg, 1926-1973—Translations,
English. I. Anderson, Mark, 1955-   . II. Title. III. Series.
PT2603.A147A23   1986   831'.912   85-43202
ISBN 0-691-06672-8   ISBN 0-691-01428-0 (pbk.)